THE INDEPE?
DISNEYLAI

G. COSTA

Limit of Liability and Disclaimer of Warranty:
The publisher has used its best efforts in preparing this book, and the information provided herein is provided "as is." Independent Guides and the author make no representation or warranties with respect to the accuracy or completeness of the contents of this book and specifically disclaims any implied warranties of merchantability or fitness for any particular purpose and shall in no event be liable for any loss of profit or any other commercial damage, including but not limited to special, incidental, consequential, or other damages.

Please read all signs before entering attractions, as well as the terms and conditions of any third party companies used. Prices are approximate, and do fluctuate.

Contents

Introduction

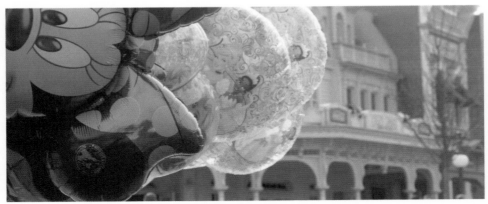

Disneyland Paris is Europe's most popular destination, having amassed over 300 million visitors in the last 27 years.

The project for the resort started in the 1980s when Disney executives wanted to bring the magic of Disney theme parks to Europe where the original stories, which inspire many Disney fairy tales, originated.

They soon decided on constructing the resort in France due to its central location and favourable weather when compared to some countries further north in Europe.

The fact that the site was less than a two-hour flight from many European locations sealed the deal - and the French government

promising to build infrastructure to access the resort.

Disneyland Park opened in 1992 as a European adaptation of California's Disneyland. Its design was, however, updated to reflect the local culture and to take advantage of all the land the company had purchased.

In 2002, Walt Disney Studios Park became the second park at the resort, providing a portal for movie fanatics.

As well as the two theme parks, guests can enjoy the Disney Village area (free admission), with shopping and dining experiences that cover a range of tastes.

A golf course, a campsite with an adventure playground, and six themed

hotels are also on site. Disneyland Paris is not just a theme park or a place to ride roller coasters. Guests can meet characters, watch shows and parades, make new friends and enjoy an ambience that no other theme park resort in Europe rivals. Thrill seekers may not find the tallest and fastest rides in Europe at the resort, but the quality of the experiences offered is second to none.

2020 is a fantastic time to visit as the resort continues to innovate.

Disneyland Paris is a place where dreams really do come true for guests every single day, and you are about to become one of them.

Planning

Planning a trip to Disneyland Paris may seem daunting. You have to think about transport, accommodation, food, park tickets, spending money, and more. This section aims to get you prepared.

When to Visit

Crowds at Disneyland Paris vary significantly from season to season and even day to day. The difference in a single day can save you hundreds of euros and hours in queues. You need to consider national and school holidays in France and surrounding countries, the weather, pricing and more to find the best time to go. Here is our guide of the best times to visit Disneyland Paris, even including a detailed analysis of weekdays.

MAJOR HOLIDAYS (TIMES TO AVOID):

Second part of 2019
• 15th June to 9th September: European School Summer Break. August is by far the busiest month. July is busier than June. September is less busy from the 2nd onwards.
• 14th July: Bastille Day (Bank Holiday)
• 15th August: Assumption
• Weekends in September: and October: Very busy
• 20th October to 3rd November: School Holidays and Halloween
• 11th November - Armistace Day
• 22nd December 2019 to 5th January 2020 - Christmas Holidays. 31st Dec is the busiest day.

In 2020
• 1st to 5th January: New

Year's Day & School Break
• 9th February to 8th March: French and UK school break
• 17th March: St. Patrick's Day (celebrations mean slightly larger crowds)
• 5th April to 3rd May: Easter Holidays - Particularly busy from 6th to 19th April.
• 1st to 3rd May: Labour Day weekend
• 8th to 10th May: Victory in Europe Day weekend
• 21st to 24th May: Ascension Day weekend
• 30th and 31st May: Pentecost/Whit Sunday
• 15th June to 6th September: European School Summer Break. August is by far the busiest month. July is busier than June. September is less busy from the 4th onwards.
• 14th July: Bastille Day

(Bank Holiday)
• 15th August: Assumption
• September and October weekends
• 17th October to 1st November: UK and France school holidays, Halloween
• 11th November - Armistace Day
• 19nd December 2020 to 4th January 2021 - Christmas Holidays. 31st Dec is the busiest day.

Top Tip: If a public holiday falls on a Friday or a Monday, that weekend becomes a *pont* (a long weekend). If it is on a Thursday or Tuesday, many turn this into a 4-day weekend. Avoid *ponts* as they are always very busy.

DAYS OF THE WEEK:

The days of the week that you visit make a large difference to how long you will wait to get on rides. A ride can have a wait time of 90 minutes on one day, and just 30 minutes the next. The most notable difference is between weekends and weekdays.

The best day of the week to visit is Monday, followed by Tuesday, then Thursday, then Wednesday, Friday and Sunday - the busiest day of the week is by far Saturday. Park hours are often extended on weekends to compensate for the larger crowds.

Doing Disney on a Budget

A visit to Disneyland Paris is expensive – it is a premium theme park destination and with travel, park tickets, accommodation, food and souvenirs, it is easy to see why many families save up for a long time for a visit. However, there are many ways to reduce your spending at the resort yet still have a magical time.

1. Drive – Visitors from all across Europe can drive to the resort. Even from the UK, driving is an option - a ferry or Eurotunnel crossing can cost as little as £50-£150 return when booked in advance for a car and all its passengers. From Calais, in France, is it an easy 3-hour drive. There are about €18-€22 of tolls each way depending on the route from Calais to Disneyland Paris, plus petrol costs.

2. Budget flights – Flights are available from £30/€40 each way from across Europe to Paris. *Charles de Gaulle* airport is the most convenient, followed by *Orly*. Steer clear of *Paris Beauvais-Tille* Airport, which is 120km away from the parks.

3. Take the train – TGV and Eurostar trains can get you to the resort. If travelling across France, try Ouigo (www.ouigo.com), which offers cheap travel on high-speed trains from locations across France.

TGV advance 'Prems' fares are also often good value.

You will arrive at *Marne la Vallée – Chessy* station.

For UK guests, Eurostar trains start at £72 return if booked in advance. Those from UK regions can book "through fares" from their home station to Disneyland Paris on Eurostar.com, changing trains at St. Pancras. For example, Manchester to Paris starts at £90 return.

Trains avoid airport transfers, saving money.

4. Hotels – Disney hotels are themed but are also expensive compared to other nearby hotels, such as the Kyriad, which have offers from €60 per night. However, a non-Disney hotel means no Extra Magic Time and buying park tickets separately.

Alternatively, stay at a cheaper Disney hotel such as the Hotel Cheyenne or Santa Fe to get the on-site benefits.

5. Buy an annual pass – If visiting for at least four days, an annual pass can work out cheaper than a 4-day ticket and you get additional dining and merchandise discounts.

6. Use a special offer – There is always a special offer running, whether it is 'kids go free', or an extra day and night free. If there are no offers, don't book and wait for one.

7. Tickets – If you are not staying at a Disney hotel, pre-purchase your tickets. Buying them at the ticket booths on the day is costly and very time-consuming.

8. Eat at Disney Village – McDonald's in Disney Village sells fast-food at prices much cheaper than food in the theme parks. Or try the well-priced Earl of Sandwich next door. Vapiano also offers a well-priced, tasty Italian meal.

9. Meal vouchers – If you are eating at restaurants daily, then pre-purchasing meal vouchers can save you money. They can be added at the time of booking or any time before your trip if staying at a Disney hotel. Vouchers must be purchased for the entire stay.

10. Packed lunches – Make your own packed lunches. There is a huge supermarket called Auchan in nearby *Val d'Europe*. Alternatively, bring food and snacks from home.

11. Take your own photos – If you do not want to pay €15 for a character photo, take one yourself;

the Cast Members do not mind. They will even take the photo for you if you ask. If you want official photos, see our section on Disneyland Paris' Photopass and Photopass+ services for unlimited photos for a set price instead of paying €15 for each one.

12. Take your own merchandise – Buy dresses, outfits and toys outside of Disneyland Paris from Disney Stores, online or

at supermarkets before you visit Disneyland Paris. Give your child the costume once you arrive to avoid the inflated in-park merchandise prices.

13. More affordable meals – Although food prices are high, some restaurants offer better value than others. Try the set menus with a main course, dessert and drink for one price. Or, try a buffet as a late lunch and have a lighter dinner.

Speaking French

All Cast Members at the resort speak French. With very few exceptions, all Cast Members at the resort also speak English.

Therefore, for the most part, the language barrier is not a problem when talking to Cast Members.

However, knowing the basics in French is helpful, and employees do appreciate it if you say *Bonjour* and then switch to English, or even better say *Parlez-vous Anglais?* [*pronounced par-lay-voo-zarn-glay*] for "Do you speak English?".

You may occasionally come across a Cast Member with a limited grasp of the English language, which can make things more difficult but not impossible. Cast Members do speak many other languages too – Spanish and Italian are common.

USEFUL FRENCH PHRASES:

Hello/Good morning – *Bonjour [Bon-sjur]*
Good evening – *Bonsoir [Bon-swar]*
Do you speak English? – *Parlez-vous anglais? [Par-lay voo-zarn-glay]*
How much does this cost? – *Ça coûte combien? [Sar Coot Com-byer]*
Please – *S'il vous plait [Sill voo-play]*
Thanks – *Merci! [Mair-si]*
No problem – *De rien [De ree-yeah]*
A photo of us, please? – *Une photo s'il vous plaît? [Oon photo sill voo-play]*
Yes – *Oui [We]*
No – *Non [No – do not pronounce the final 'n']*
A little / a bit – *Un peu [Um purr]*
Rare (for meat) – *Saignante [Say-narnte]*
Medium-Rare (for meat) – *À pointe [Ah pwarnt]*
Well-done/well-cooked (for meat) – *Bien Cuite [Bee-yen kweet]*
Very well-cooked (for meat) – *Très Bien Cuite [Treh bee-yen kweet]*

Currency and Payment Methods

France uses Euros as its currency. If you come from a country that does not use Euros as its currency, then you can either exchange cash before you go, or use a debit/credit card while in France.

With payment cards, be aware that many banks add additional fees when paying in a foreign currency.

Be sure to warn your bank you will be travelling to avoid your card being blocked for security reasons.

Traveller's cheques are accepted at Disneyland Paris, but we do not recommend these.

We recommend using a Pre-paid debit card from a company such as FairFX (UK readers only, but other similar companies are available in other countries).

These pre-paid cards allow you to top-up the card with Euros, like a mobile phone top up. You can then use the card for purchases with no additional fees when abroad and recharge the card at any time.

FairFx usually charges a £9.95 card purchase fee. However, if you use our special link at http://bit.ly/debitdlp - the card purchase fee magically disappears. Our exclusive link also includes bonus

cash for top-ups over £250.

For guests who prefer to exchange money at the theme parks, there are Bureau de Changes located at both theme parks and in the Disney Village. These operate limited opening hours and the rates offered are usually quite poor.

Celebrating Birthdays

There are several ways to celebrate a birthday at Disneyland Paris. For example, at Table Service restaurants, you can add a birthday cake to your meal for €35.

We recommend making a restaurant reservation by calling the dining booking line and mentioning the cake in advance - you can do this up to 2 months before the big day.

Additionally, guests can visit City Hall and Studio Services to be given a 'Happy Birthday' badge to wear throughout the day.

To entertain younger guests, make sure to ask the Cast Members at City Hall whether any of the characters have a special birthday message for your child.

You will enter a room where a phone will ring, and when your child picks the phone up, there will be a recorded message wishing them a happy birthday – this can make for some incredible memories.

Getting There

Travelling to Disneyland Paris is simple due to its central location. Options include driving, flying and high-speed trains.

Plane

Flying to Paris is convenient for many visitors as the French capital is under two hours away from most of Europe, and in the era of budget airlines, flying doesn't have to break the bank either. Paris has three airports you fly into:

Charles-de-Gaulle Airport
This is the main Parisian airport and the largest.

o *By High-Speed TGV Train*: From the airport, catch a direct TGV train which takes between 9 and 12 minutes from *Terminal 2* to *Marne-La-Vallee – Chessy (Disneyland)* station. You can pre-book online if you wish at www.voyages-sncf.com. Tickets are €19 to €35 per person each way. The first train is at about 07:00; there are no direct TGV trains after 21:16 (check the schedule online by making a test booking). We recommend buying tickets at the airport instead of pre-booking for a specific timed train.

o *By Local RER Train*: From the airport, get the RER B to *Chatelet les Halles* station, then switch to RER A to *Marne La Vallée – Chessy*. This costs €17.30 per adult with a travel time of about 1 hour 30 minutes. Children under 10 years of age pay €10.65, and children under 4 travel free.

o *By Coach*: The Magical Shuttle bus goes between the airport and Disneyland Paris and even to many Val d'Europe hotels. There are up to 22 journeys in each direction daily. Pricing is €23

per adult each way and €10 per child ages 3 to 11. The journey takes about 1 hour and 35 minutes each way. Book at magicalshuttle.co.uk.

o *By Taxi*: A taxi costs €90 to €100 each way. This is a well-priced and convenient option for groups.

Orly Airport
Paris' second largest airport.

o *By Coach*: The Magical Shuttle bus is €23 per adult each way, children pay €10. Coach transfers take approximately 1 hour and 35 minutes each way. Book at magicalshuttle.co.uk.

o *By Local RER Train*: Get the *Orlyval* train (6:00am to 11:00pm) to *Antony Orlyval* station. From *Antony Orlyval*, take the RER B to *Chatelet-Les Halles* station. There, get the RER A to *Marne la vallée – Chessy (Disneyland)* station. The total journey time is 1 hour and 30 minutes. Price: €19.35 per adult and €14.25 per child.

o *By Taxi/Private Van*: Prices are €80 to €135 for parties of 3 to 8 people. This is the cheapest and most comfortable choice for groups.

Paris Beauvais-Tille Airport
This airport is not in Paris despite its marketing efforts and therefore has long transfer times.

o *By Public Transport*: Get a shuttle bus from *Beauvais Airport* to *Porte Maillot* bus station. This is €16 one-way or €29 return per adult (for children ages 4-11 the price is €10 and €20). This shuttle bus journey takes 1 hour 15 minutes. At *Porte Maillot*, follow the signs to the Metro and take Line 1 (yellow) to *La Defense* (10 minutes). At *La Defense* take the RER A line (red) to *Marne La Vallée – Chessy Disneyland* station (50 to 60 minutes – €7.60 per adult, €3.80 per child). The total journey time is about 2 hours 30 minutes, plus transfer time and the total cost is about €25 per person.

o By Shuttle Service: SuperShuttle.fr provides a shared shuttle from the airport to Disneyland Paris for €65 per person, or €185 for a non-stop shuttle for up to 8 passengers. The journey time is about 1 hour 30 minutes.

o *By Taxi*: The taxi fare is approximately €180 to €200 each way. You can alternatively rent a car. The journey is 126km each way.

Train

The Eurostar is the most comfortable option for visitors from the south of the UK, reaching the doorstep of Disneyland Paris in just 2 hours 49 minutes from London, and even more quickly from Ebbsfleet and Ashford. Prices start at £72 (€88) per adult return.

Direct from the UK:
There is one direct train per day that leaves London at 10:14 and arrives at 14:03 at *Marne la Vallée-Chessy* Station (Disneyland).

Return direct trains depart Disneyland Paris at either 16:55 or 18:01 depending on the day of the week. There are no direct trains on Tuesdays, Thursdays and Saturdays, except during British school holidays.

The direct Eurostar service is incredibly convenient with security, immigration and check-in usually done in less than fifteen minutes.

Indirect via Lille:
As there is an only one direct Eurostar service per day (and none on some days), you may want to use the indirect option, giving you more flexibility for times. It is also often cheaper than the direct train.

Passengers board a Eurostar train in the UK (usually with the destination of Brussels) and disembark at *Lille Europe* station - about 1 hour and 20 minutes from London. At *Lille Europe*, passengers wait for their connecting TGV train from *Lille Europe* to *Marne la Vallée - Chessy* Station (Disneyland).

The whole journey takes as little as 2h53m from London with a 28-minute stopover. Some stopovers are longer, however, so your journey may take up to 4 hours 8 minutes.

The Eurostar website does not usually show indirect trains more than 12 weeks in advance.

Changing trains is easy - you look for the number of your next train on the departure board and head to that platform. Thirty minutes is plenty of time to change, as there are no security or immigration checks here. When on the platform itself, do check that you are on the right train, as there may be multiple trains on the same platform.

The TGV train from *Lille - Europe* makes several stops and only stops at *Marne-La-Vallee - Chessy (Disneyland)* for a few minutes - make sure not to miss your stop, as it is not the end of the route.

There is a helpful video of this process available from 'Disneyland Paris Advice' called "Eurostar indirect via Lille" on Youtube. You can find this video directly at http://bit.ly/dlplillechange.

TOP TIP
Do not book your Eurostar travel with Disneyland Paris as part of a package without checking prices direct with Eurostar. It often works out significantly more expensive to book transportation with Disneyland Paris. We usually recommend booking your train directly at www.eurostar.com. However, when Disney has an offer such as free travel for children, it can be significantly cheaper to book with Disneyland Paris. As such, we recommend you check both options.

You can book Eurostar trains between 3 and 6 months in advance, depending on the season and route.

International Train + RER (via central Paris):
Disneyland Paris is about 32km from central Paris, and the city centre is connected to the theme park by the fast and frequent RER train service.

Therefore, you can easily get a high-speed international train to Paris, followed by a local RER train to Disneyland Paris.

This offers you a lot of flexibility – for example, there are up to 18 Eurostar departures per day from London to Paris.

When you arrive at *Paris – Gare du Nord* station by Eurostar, it will take a further 50 to 60 minutes to reach Disneyland Paris.

At the time of writing, a ticket on the Paris RER train from *Gare du Nord* to *Marne-La-Vallée (Disneyland Paris)* costs €7.60 per adult and €3.80 for a child under 10 years old.

Follow the signs at *Gare du Nord* for 'Metro and RER' trains.

Take the RER B line in the direction of *Robinson, Antony* or *Saint Rémy-lès-Chevreuse* for one stop to *Chatelet-Les Halles*. Here you transfer to RER A by walking to the other side of the platform and getting a train in the direction of *Marne La Vallée – Chessy*.

Use the overhead information boards to verify that the train is going to *Marne La Vallée – Chessy station* (your destination). If it will be stopping at Disneyland, there should be a light illuminated next to the station's name. *Marne La Vallée - Chessy (Disneyland)* is the last stop on the RER A line. This journey takes about 40 minutes.

DISNEY EXPRESS

If you have booked your train as part of a package, you will have the Disney Express luggage transfer service included. This allows you to drop off your bags at the train station and make the most of your time in the parks.

At *Marne-La-Vallee* Station, follow the signs to the Disney Express counters on the top floor (8:00 am to 9:30 pm daily).

Here, you check in for your hotel, receive park tickets, meal vouchers (if ordered) and other bits. Leave your bags with the Cast Members at these desks and they will be taken to the luggage storage area in your hotel. Now, explore the parks!

This service is available on both direct and indirect Eurostar services, as well as for guests arriving via TGV at *Marne La Vallée - Chessy* station.

If you booked your train separately, this service costs €15 per person each way.

Driving

You have two options to reach Disneyland Paris if driving from the UK.

The Eurotunnel is a train service that allows passengers and vehicles to travel together from Folkestone (England) and arrive in Calais (France) in 35 minutes.

Alternatively, you can take your car on the ferry from Dover (England) to Calais (France). P&O Ferries is a popular company. The ferry crossing is often cheaper than the Eurotunnel but takes about 90 minutes, almost three times as long as the train.

From Calais (France) it is a 3 hour 30 minute drive to Disneyland Paris. Take the A26 towards Arras passing through St. Omer.

There, take the A1 (also known as *Autoroute du Nord* or E15) towards Paris. Take exit 6 after Charles de Gaulle Airport, onto the A104. This will take you to the A4, follow this road. Exit 14 is Disneyland.

This 290km (180 mi) journey will cost approximately €18 to €22 in tolls and approximately €30 to €40 in fuel each way.

Hotels

Disneyland Paris owns and operates seven on-site resort hotels, each themed to a different part of America – one is even a campsite where you can stay in log cabins. When booking a hotel directly with Disneyland Paris, your hotel price also includes your park entry tickets.

Advantages of staying at a Disneyland Paris hotel:
• A front desk staffed 24 hours a day
• Friendly Cast Members with knowledge of the resort
• Make dining reservations in person without needing to leave your hotel
• The option to pre-pay for all your meals at the hotel and the theme parks.
• Detailed theming and total immersion
• A stay in the heart of the Disney magic
• Extra Magic Times available daily. EMTs allow hotel guests entry into selected parts of both parks one hour before other guests. During EMT attraction wait times are very short or non-existent.
• Walking distance to the theme parks: 20 minutes or less.
• Free shuttle service from all the hotels to the theme parks (except Disney's Davy Crockett Ranch)
• The opportunity to meet Disney characters at the hotel throughout your stay.
• Disney Shopping Service: If you buy merchandise in the parks before 3:00pm, you can have it delivered to your hotel to be collected in the evening, leaving your hands free.
• Park admission tickets are included in all reservations unless otherwise stated.

Pricing:

When booking your hotel, your arrival date determines the price for your entire stay (e.g. if you arrive on a date within the Value pricing season and the remaining days of your holiday are in the Moderate pricing season, your whole stay will be charged at the Value price).

However, this can also work against you where your arrival date could be in High season and then your other nights in the Regular season. In this case, you will pay the High season rate for the entire duration.

There are two solutions:

change your dates, or book one package for the more expensive night(s) and then another separate package for the cheaper remaining night(s). You may have to leave your room and re-check in if you do this. If you book two back-to-back stays, ask the Cast Member checking you in whether you can keep the same room.

To see what season you will arrive in, download the brochure and price grid from disneylandparis.com. A booking agent may be able to advise what the best option for you is if you book over the phone.

MORE ON PRICING

Room prices in this section are based on arrivals until 1st April 2020. Prices listed are per night and include park tickets for all days of your stay, including check in and check out days.

Prices are per person per night for a standard room based on two adults sharing; so 2 adults will need to double the price per night listed. A single adult in a room will need to pay a nightly supplement — additional adults after the second pay a nightly surcharge.

Children under 3 always stay free; children 3 to 11 pay a child price, but there are often sales where this fee is waived for kids.

Multiple-night stays carry a lower "per night" cost. The per-night cost after the third night is 45% to 85% cheaper, as most visitors will not need more than four days to visit the resort. This can make an extended stay at the hotels much better value for money overall.

Magic Card:
The Magic Card is exclusive to the seven Disneyland Paris operated hotels and is given to guests at check-in.

It allows you entry to the theme parks during Extra Magic Times, access to the hotel pools, and free parking both at the hotel and the theme park parking lot, as well as acting as your room key and meal plan voucher.

During check-in, you can also link a credit or debit card to your Magic Card, which will allow you to pay for food and merchandise at most resort locations using the Magic Card instead of paying with your credit card or in cash each time. You then settle the bill when checking out and pay one lump sum.

This can be a good option for guests from non-euro countries whose credit banks charge a per-transaction foreign currency fee. Just be sure to monitor your spending to not go over budget.

Note: Some small stalls (such as those selling drinks or popcorn) do not accept the Magic Card or credit/debit cards, and only take cash. Disney does not operate restaurants in Disney Village, so these are unlikely to accept the Magic Card – but do ask.

How to book your stay:
We recommend booking Disneyland Paris hotels or packages through the official website at www.disneylandparis.com.

The website offers you several room types, but suites must be booked over the phone. Both the Disneyland Paris website and phone reservations charge a £25 booking fee.

Disneyland Paris regularly runs promotions with savings of 10-50% off the regular price, or 'get free nights' deals when you book a stay. If there is not a sale when you are thinking of booking, we recommend waiting as sales run throughout the entire year.

Offers vary seasonally and between different countries. These can be anything from 'free hotel, park tickets and transport for under 12s' to 'free half board meal plans', or even 40% or 50% off a stay. A minimum stay of two or three nights usually applies to promotions, as well as date restrictions.

BOOKING TIPS

Tip 1: You can book Disneyland Paris (and partner) hotels over the phone. Phone booking allows you to pay in instalments instead of one lump sum, with no interest. This allows you to modify your reservation up until you have paid the full amount. So, if a better offer becomes available after you book, you can make changes until the final balance is paid, such as upgrading your hotel or adding meal vouchers.

Tip 2: Disneyland Paris runs different promotions in different areas of Europe simultaneously. The good news is you can book any of the promotions from any country. Visit www.disneylandparis.com - at the top of the page select another country, and then try booking through there. You will pay in the currency local to that country. The website's language may also change when you do this. You can also do this by calling Disneyland Paris directly and stating the offer you would like to use.

Here is an example of the different promotions available at the time of writing this guide. The UK Disneyland Paris website offered 30% off stays, and the Spanish website offered 25% off stays, a €200 gift card and kids go free under age 7. Clearly, these are very different offers with different savings depending on your needs.

Disneyland Hotel

This 565-room, 27-suite, Art Deco/Victorian Hotel is the height of luxury at Disneyland Paris. It is located at the entrance of Disneyland Park and just 3 minutes away from the Studios.

The Disneyland Hotel is the most expensive and luxurious place to stay on Disneyland Paris property.

The hotel adorns the entrance of Disneyland Park, with the park's turnstiles underneath it. Some of the rooms have views over Disneyland Park, or over the Fantasia Gardens area in front of the hotel.

The hotel has numerous dining options, including a buffet restaurant (Inventions), an upscale dining experience (California Grill) and a bar (Cafe Fantasia).

From California Grill, you can watch the nightly fireworks from the balcony if you time your dinner right.

The Celestia Spa is open from 2:00pm to 9:00pm daily. Facials start at €95 and body treatments from €55. Massages start at €60

for 20 minutes. There are even kids spa experiences for €60. Reservations are recommended and can be made in person or by calling 6605 from hotel room phones or +33 1 60 45 66 05.

Guests staying in the Disneyland Hotel's Castle Club or suites get one VIP Fastpass per person valid for their entire stay. It allows unlimited any-time entry into every Fastpass attraction at both parks.

Castle Club rooms are club level and offer numerous benefits. Castle Club guests may access a private bar area with complimentary non-alcoholic beverages throughout the day, and a perfect view of the fireworks through the windows with the music piped in at night.

There are also characters present in the morning and sometimes the evening at the Castle Club. There

is even a private lift from Castle Club directly to the turnstiles without walking through the rest of the hotel. This is a truly unique, premium experience.

A 'Princess or Pirate for a Day' experience is available for all guests, including those not staying at the hotel. Your little boy or girl can be transformed into a piraate or princess with a costume, accessories and more. Pricing is €105.

The Club Minnie Playroom is open from 2:00pm to 9:00pm, with activities for children. The games room/arcade is open from 8:00am to 1:00am.

Room size: 34m^2 for standard rooms (up to 4 people, plus one child under 3 years old in a cot), and 58m^2 in the Castle Club Suites (other suites go up to 187m^2 – including the Sleeping Beauty suite, the Cinderella suite, Tinker Bell suite and Walt's Apartment Suite). Family rooms (up to 5 people with one on a sofa bed), and Castle Club rooms (up to 4 people – phone bookings only) are also available.

Breakfast: Extra charge. €30 per day per adult and €27 per child.

Room Prices: 1 night is €435 to €722, 2 nights is €757 to €1331, 3 nights is €1075 to €1936. Additional nights are between €339 and €626. A Castle Club room is priced at an additional €160 to €250 per person per night.

Activities: An indoor pool, sauna, steam bath and a fitness suite are all complimentary for guests. A spa with a massage service is available for an extra fee. A "Club Minnie" Playroom, children's corner, and a video game arcade are also available. Dry cleaning is available at a surcharge.

Extras: Free Wi-Fi is available throughout the hotel, including guests' rooms.

DINING:

Inventions – Buffet service. Lunch with Disney characters from 12:30pm to 3:00pm (Adults: €69, drinks not included; Children: €39 with one drink included). Dinner with Disney characters is from 6:00pm to 10:30pm daily (Adults: €69, drinks not included; Children: €39 with one drink included). Additionally, a themed Brunch is served with the Disney Characters from 1:00pm to 3:00pm every Sunday (Adults: €99, Children: €45). Selected offerings at this restaurant are included in the Premium Meal Plan and the Hotel Meal Plan.

California Grill – Table Service. Starters are €20 to €35. Main courses are €42 to €66. Desserts are €20 to €28. Set menus vary from €70 to €130 for adults; €36 for children. Disney states, "A chic and casual style suits the place. Shoulders must be covered for men. Bermuda shorts, shorts and flip flops are not permitted.." Open for dinner only. Some offerings at this restaurant are available on the Premium Meal Plan.

Café Fantasia – Hotel Bar, serving drinks and snacks. Cocktails are €16-€19, champagne (75ml) is priced at €65-€310, other wines (75ml) are €37-€200, soft drinks are €6-€8 and hot drinks are €6.50-€7.

Disney's Hotel New York - The Art of Marvel

This Art Deco, New York-themed hotel features 565 rooms and 27 suites, and is a mere 10-minute walk to the parks. A shuttle bus is also available.

TOP TIP

Disney's Hotel New York is closed until summer 2020. It is currently going through a large-scale refurbishment and re-theming to have Marvel influences throughout. An exact opening date is not available.

Themed to an apartment block in the Big Apple, this is the second closest hotel to the parks, and is located by the entrance of Disney Village and Lake Disney.

This hotel is closed until summer 2020. The information on this page refers to pricing and amenities before the refurbishment, and these will likely change upon reopening.

Room size: 31m² in standard rooms (for 4 people). Empire State Club lodging includes Club Rooms and Club Suites (ranging between 56m² and 166m²).

Breakfast: Extra charge. €25 per day per adult and €23 per child.
Room Prices: 1 night is €269 to €429, 2 nights is €426 to €746, 3 nights is €588 to €1068. Extra nights are €122 to €282. For Empire State Club rooms, add an extra €70 to €80 per person per night.

Activities: Complimentary heated outdoor and indoor pools, sauna and/or steam bath, tennis courts and gym. Massages are available for a fee. There is an on-site hairdresser available to hotel and non-hotel guests. A kids' play area and a games arcade are available.
Extras: Free Wi-Fi access throughout the hotel, including rooms. Dry cleaning is available. Suite guests get one VIP Fastpass per person valid for their stay, with unlimited entry into every Fastpass attraction. Guests staying in the Empire State Club Rooms get one Hotel Fastpass per day, allowing immediate entry to the Fastpass queue line to one attraction.

DINING:

Manhattan Restaurant – Table Service. Main courses are €21 to €33. Set menus are €36 to €56 for adults, and €30 for kids. Some options are included in the Premium Meal Plan and the Plus Meal Plan.
Parkside Diner – Continental breakfast is available. Dinner buffet (18:00 to 23:00) is €35 for adults without a drink, and €19 for kids with one drink. The buffets are on both the Hotel and Plus Meal Plans.
New York City Bar – Bar. Snacks from 11:30am to 3:00pm including sandwiches for €12.50 and pasta salads for €13.

Disney's Newport Bay Club:

This New-England style hotel features 1093 rooms and 13 suites. It is a 15-minute walk to the parks, or a free shuttle bus journey away.

Themed to New England, this nautical-inspired hotel houses two restaurants and anchors one end of lake Disney. It is the fourth closest hotel to the parks and was recently refurbished.

Room size: Standard rooms are 27m²; family rooms for up to 6 guests are also available. Suites include Admiral's Floor at 27m², Honeymoon Suites from 50m² to 63m², The Resort Suite at 55m² and the Presidential Suite measuring 84m².

Breakfast: Extra charge. €25 per day per adult and €23 per child.

Room Prices: 1 night is €275 to €435, 2 nights is €437 to €757, 3 nights is €595 to €1075. Extra nights are €180 to €340. For Compass Club rooms, add an extra €80 to €85 per person per night.

Activities: Indoor and outdoor pools, with deckchairs; sauna/steam bath; and fitness suite. Massages are an extra charge. There is an indoor kids play area.

Extras: Free Wi-Fi access throughout the hotel and in guest rooms. This hotel has a convention centre. Dry cleaning is available at a surcharge.

Guests staying in one the suites (not Compass Club) get one VIP Fastpass per person valid for their stay. This allows unlimited entry into every Fastpass attraction.

Guests in the Compass club get one Hotel Fastpass per day, allowing immediate entry to the Fastpass queue to one attraction.

DINING:

Yacht Club – Table Service. Main courses are €31 to €56. Adult set menus are €47 to €56, €26 and €33 for kids. Some meals are in the Premium & Plus Meal Plans.
Cape Cod – Buffet. €37 for adults with no drinks, €25 for children with one drink. Some meals at this restaurant are in the Hotel and Plus Meal Plans.
Captain's Quarters – Hotel Bar, serving drinks and snacks.

Disney's Sequoia Lodge

Recreating the ambience of the American National Parks, the Sequoia Lodge's 1011 rooms and 14 suites are a 15-minute walk from the parks. A shuttle is also available.

Disney's Sequoia Lodge is our favourite on-site hotel as far as value for money is concerned.

It is a mid-priced hotel, but it is slightly closer to the parks than the more expensive Newport Bay Club Hotel. In addition, we feel this hotel is one of the best themed on property. There is nothing better than snuggling up next to the huge fireplace in the Redwood Bar and Lounge in the winter.

Room size: 22m^2 in a standard room. Golden Forest Club rooms (with a private lounge with snacks) are also available, as are Honeymoon Suites and Hospitality Suites (55m^2).

Breakfast: Extra charge. €19 per day per adult and €17 per child.

Room Prices: 1 night is €241 to €379, 2 nights is €369 to €645, 3 nights is €493 to €907. Additional nights are €145 to €283. Golden Forest rooms are an extra €55 to €70 per person per night.

Activities: Indoor and outdoor pool; fitness suite; sauna/steam bath. Massages are available for an extra charge. Kids play areas are also available.

Extras: Free Wi-Fi access throughout the hotel, including in rooms.

Guests staying in a suite get one VIP Fastpass per person valid for all their stay. This allows unlimited entry into all Fastpass attractions.

Guests staying in the Golden Forest Club Rooms get one Hotel Fastpass per day, allowing immediate entry to the Fastpass queue line to one attraction.

DINING:

Hunter's Grill and **Beaver Creek Tavern**– Buffet menu priced at €37 without drinks for an adult, and €25 with one drink for children.

Redwood Bar and Lounge – Hotel Bar and Lounge.

Disney's Hotel Cheyenne

Themed to America's Old Wild West, with details from the Toy Story films, this 1000 room hotel is a 20-minute walk from the parks. A shuttle is also available.

The Cheyenne, along with the Santa Fe, are the resort's budget hotels and provide the best value for money. The rooms and services on offer are more basic than the other hotels, but you still have access to Extra Magic Times, and you can walk to the parks (or get a complimentary shuttle).

In terms of overall theming, we feel that this is one of the most well-themed hotels with the buildings shaped to look like they are part of the Wild West.

Room size: Standard rooms measure 21m^2.

Breakfast: Extra charge. €19 per day per adult and €14 per child.

Room Prices: 1 night is priced at €220 to €346, 2 nights is €327 to €579, 3 nights is €430 to €808.

Additional nights are priced at €125 to €250.

Activities: Video games room; outdoor and indoor kids play areas; seasonal pony rides are available for an added charge. There is no pool at this hotel.

Extras: Free Wi-Fi is available at the bar and in the lobby only. Wi-Fi is not available in guest rooms at the time of writing.

DINING:

Chuck Wagon Café – Buffet. Continental breakfast (7:00am to 11:00am) is available. Dinner (6:00pm to 10:30pm) is a buffet – €30 with one drink, and €17 per child with a drink. The adult buffet and the child buffet are included in the Hotel and Standard Meal Plans.
Red Garter Saloon – Hotel Bar, serving snacks and drinks.
Starbucks – Snacks, Drinks - €4 to €6, sandwiches - €5, breakfast deal - €9.

Disney's Hotel Santa Fe

Themed to Santa Fe, in South West America, and with hints of Pixar's 'Cars' films. This 1000 room hotel is a 20-minute walk from the parks. A shuttle is also available.

The Santa Fe, along with Cheyenne, are Disneyland Paris' budget hotels and provide the best value for money. The rooms and services on offer are more basic than the other hotels, but you still have access to Extra Magic Times, and you can walk to the parks (or take a complimentary shuttle).

In terms of theming, this is our least favourite hotel - the buildings do resemble some in real Santa Fe, but it is not the most magical of themes. This hotel is usually slightly cheaper than the Cheyenne Hotel.

This hotel is also marginally further away than the Cheyenne Hotel. It does, however, provide a relatively affordable option to stay on-site at a Disney hotel.

Room size: A standard room measures 21m² (up to 4 people plus 1 child under 3 years in a cot). Family rooms for up to 6 people are also available.

Breakfast: Extra charge. €19 per day per adult and €14 per child.

Room Prices: 1 night is priced at €220 to €321, 2 nights is €327 to €529, 3 nights is €430 to €733. Additional nights are priced at €125 to €225.

Activities: A video game arcade is available. There is no pool at this hotel.

Extras: Free Wi-Fi available is available throughout the hotel, including in guest rooms.

DINING:

La Cantina – Buffet from 6:00pm to 10:30pm. Continental breakfast is available. Buffet: €31 with a drink, and €17 per child. The adult and child buffets are included in Standard Meal Plan.

Rio Grande Bar – Hotel Bar.

Starbucks – Snacks, Drinks - €4 to €6, sandwiches - €5, breakfast deal - €9.

Disney's Davy Crockett Ranch

Unlike the other Disney properties, the Davy Crockett Ranch is not a hotel, but a 595-cabin campsite.

Davy Crockett Ranch is unlike any of the other accommodation covered in this section. It is not a standard hotel, but a campsite. Here you do not stay in a hotel room, but a large log cabin instead.

You truly do feel a world away from the theme parks in a serene environment. This accommodation is best for large groups with rooms for up to 6 people.

Davy Crockett Ranch is not located near any of the other on-site hotels, and is further than any of the partner hotels too. It is an 8km (15-minute) drive by car to the parks - you must provide your own transport as shuttle buses are not available.

Room size: There are both 1-bedroom (36m²) and 2-bedroom (39m²) cabins available. Cabins house up to 6 people. A Premium 2-bedroom cabin option is also available.

Breakfast: Extra charge.

Room prices: 1 night is priced at €222 to €311, 2 nights is €331 to €509, 3 nights is €436 to €703 for a standard bungalow. Additional nights are €126 to €215.

Activities: There is a beautiful heated indoor swimming pool at this resort, as well as tennis courts, a video games arcade, pony rides, quad bikes, indoor and outdoor children's play areas, a small farm and an adventure ropes course (Davy's Crockett Adventure). Some activities require a surcharge.

Extras: Free Wi-Fi is available at the restaurant and the bar. In-room wired internet access is available at a surcharge. Daily cleaning of cabins is an extra charge. The Alamo Trading Post shop sells food, clothes and souvenirs.

DINING:

Davy Crockett's Tavern – Buffet. Meals are priced at €31 per adult and €17 per child.
Crockett's Saloon – Hotel Bar.

Partner Hotels

Partner hotels are located just outside the main Disneyland Paris resort land but are often much more affordable than Disney's hotels. Sample room prices are supplied by Disneyland Paris and include theme park tickets. You can also book these hotels independently without park tickets.

❶ Radisson Blu Hotel

Number of rooms: 250 guest rooms and suites.
Room Size: Standard room (30m², maximum occupancy: 2 adults and 1 child aged under 3), Family room (30m², maximum occupancy: up to 4 adults), Junior Suite (60m²), Suite (70m²) and Presidential Suite (90m²).
Breakfast: Included in most rates.
Room Prices: Sample price per person per night (based on 2 adults per room): €267.50
Activities: Swimming pool, fitness centre, spa, and outdoor play area. By the Disneyland Paris golf course, with 9 and 18-hole courses available to play on (extra charge).
Extras: Free Wi-Fi is throughout the hotel, including in rooms. Meeting rooms available.
Dining: Pamplemousse – French Table Service; Birdie – Buffet; and Le Chardon – Bar.

❷ Vienna House Dream Castle Hotel

Number of rooms: 397 rooms and suites.
Room Size: Double rooms and family rooms (28m²), double queen rooms (44m²), Rapunzel suite (54m²), The Baron von Münchhausen Suite (60m²) and The Royal Suite (220m²).
Breakfast: Included in most rates.
Room Prices: Sample price per person per night (based on 2 adults per room): €223.50
Activities: Swimming pool, fitness centre, spa, indoor and outdoor play area, carousel, and a video game room.
Extras: Free Wi-Fi is available throughout the hotel, including in guest rooms.
Dining: Les Trois Mosquetaires – Buffet; and Excalibur – Bar.

❸ Vienna House Magic Circus Hotel

Number of rooms: 396 rooms and suites.
Room Size: Double rooms and family rooms (28m²), and suites (up to 60m²).
Breakfast: Included in most rates.
Room Prices: Sample price per person per night (based on 2 adults per room): €223.50
Activities: Swimming pool and fitness centre.
Extras: Free Wi-Fi is available throughout the hotel, including in guest rooms
Dining: L'Etoile – Buffet; and Bar des Artistes – Bar

❹ Adagio ApartHotel Marne la Valle - Val d'Europe

Number of rooms: 290 studios and apartments.
Room Size: Studios (21m²), 1 to 3 bedroom apartments (27m² to 53m²)
Breakfast: Included in most rates in the breakfast room.
Room Prices: Sample price per person per night (based on 2 adults per room): €206.50
Activities: Swimming pool
Extras: Free Wi-Fi throughout the hotel, including in rooms. There is no restaurant (except for the buffet breakfast). Rooms include a kitchenette to cook your own meals.

⑤ Alongquin's Explorers Hotel
Number of rooms: 390.
Room Size: Standard crew rooms measure 18m^2 to 22m^2.
Breakfast: Included in most rates.
Room Prices: Sample price per person per night (based on 2 adults per room): €233.50
Activities: Swimming pool, play areas, video games room, and kids fitness area.
Extras: Free Wi-Fi is available throughout the hotel, including in guest rooms. Themed suites are also available including Planet Hollywood, Sweet and Jungle themes.
Dining: La Plantation – Buffet; Captain's Library – Table Service; Marco's Pizza – Quick Service; and The Traders – Bar

⑥ Hotel L'Elysée - Val d'Europe
Number of rooms: 152 rooms, including 4 executive suites.
Room Size: Cosy rooms (24m^2 - 2 person limit), family rooms (24m^2 - 4 person limit), family XL rooms (up to 48m^{2}s - 8 person limit) and exec suites (38m^2 - 4 person limit).
Breakfast: Included in most rates.
Room Prices: Sample price per person per night (based on 2 adults per room): €208
Activities: No extra amenities.
Extras: Free Wi-Fi is available throughout the hotel, including in guest rooms. Meeting rooms are available. Laundry is available for an additional charge. Close to Val d'Europe RER station.
Dining: Restaurant – Table service (lunch only); and L'Etoile – Bar.

⑦ Campanile Val de France
Number of rooms: 300
Room Size: Standard rooms measure 18.5m^2 for up to 4 people.
Breakfast: Included in most rates.
Room Prices: Sample price per person per night (based on 2 adults per room): €199.50
Activities: Carousel, video games room, and indoor children's play area.
Extras: Free Wi-Fi is available throughout the hotel, including in guest rooms.
Dining: Le Marché Gourmand – Buffet; and L'Abreuvoir – Bar

⑧ B&B Hotel
Number of rooms: 400
Room Size: Standard rooms measure 15m^2 for up to 5 people.
Breakfast: Included in most rates.
Room Prices: Sample price per person per night (based on 2 adults per room): €197.50
Activities: Carousel and video games room.
Extras: Free Wi-Fi is available throughout the hotel, including in guest rooms.
Dining: Breakfast, Snack Bar and Hotel Bar

MORE ABOUT PARTNER HOTELS

There is no Disney theming at these hotels, but they are kid-friendly and staff have some knowledge of the theme parks. All these hotels provide frequent shuttle buses, and the longest shuttle bus ride is only 10 minutes. Wait times for buses may be up to 25 minutes in low seasons; buses are frequent (every 10 to 15 minutes) at peak times.

Most of the hotels also have a Disney shop where in-park purchases can be delivered. Partner hotels do not generally include city taxes when booked – these must be paid at check-in and are about €1-€2 per adult per night. If you don't wish to book a package, then use a hotel aggregator such as Hotels.com. For a package book with Disneyland Paris direct.

Tickets

There are many ways to buy park entry tickets for Disneyland Paris. Prices, special offers and ticket lengths vary depending on where you buy your tickets. To help you choose the best option for you, here is a detailed look at Disneyland Paris' ticket options.

Important: If you have booked a Disney hotel through the Disneyland Paris website or over the phone, you can skip this section, as your tickets are included in your package unless you specifically make a room-only reservation.

At the Park

Guests who turn up at Disneyland Paris spontaneously can buy tickets at the booths at the entrance of each theme park. As at the park you are a captive market, 'gate prices' (purchased on-site at Disneyland Paris) are the most expensive. You can get a substantial discount by booking in advance, and save *a lot* of time.

You can purchase one-park or two-park tickets for one or multiple days at any of the ticket booths. As well as the staffed ticket booths, there are also automated ticket booths under the Disneyland Hotel.

Disney Stores

You can buy tickets at any Disney Store in the UK for Disneyland Paris and most Disney Stores around Europe. Tickets for Disneyland Paris may also be stocked at selected other Disney Stores worldwide. Just ask at the counter. These tickets are priced at the same rate as at the theme park ticket booths, but will save you time queuing when at the resort as you can proceed directly to the turnstiles. If you are buying in advance, then we recommend you do so online to get the largest savings.

GATE TICKET PRICES

1 day/1 park
Adults: €87; Children €80

1 day/2 parks
Adults: €107; Children €100

2 days/2 parks
Adults: €169; Children €156

3 days/2 parks
Adults: €211; Children €195

4 days/2 parks
Adults: €249; Children €229

Children are classed as 3 to 11 year olds. Children under 3 enter for free – proof of age may be requested.

Gate ticket prices last increased in April 2019.

The ticket booths for Disneyland Park are located under the pink Disneyland Hotel. Ticket booths for the Walt Disney Studios Park are located to the right of the park's entrance turnstiles.

Online

If you purchase your tickets in advance online, you can make significant savings on the standard prices. The price varies depending on the date of your visit and visit length.

1-Day Tickets:
Mini Ticket
• 1 Park – Adult: €56; Child: €51
• 2 Parks – Adult: €76; Child: €71

Magic Ticket
• 1 Park – Adult: €74; Child: €68
• 2 Parks – Adult: €94; Child: €88

Super Magic Ticket
• 1 Park – Adult: €87; Child: €80
• 2 Parks – Adult: €107; Child: €100

Multi-Day Tickets:
• **2 days/2 parks**
Adult: €169; Child: €156

• **3 days/2 parks**
Adult: €211; Child: €195

• **4 days/2 parks**
Adult: €249; Child: €229

There are often ticket offers available online such as one extra day free (E.g. pay for 2 days, get 3 days), or where adults pay the price of the child ticket.

Mini, Magic and Super Magic tickets are valid on select days only.

Discounted single-day tickets bought online can be purchased up to one day prior to the date of your visit. They cannot be used on the day of purchase itself unless you buy a full priced ticket online.

If you opt to have the tickets posted to your home address (additional charges apply), the tickets must be purchased at least 10 days prior to the date of your visit.

> ## TICKET BROKERS
> There are also online ticket brokers that provide genuine discounted attraction tickets, sometimes with big savings! We recommend looking at: Attraction Tickets Direct, AttractionTix and 365Tickets.

Annual Passes

A Disneyland Paris Annual Pass gives you a year of benefits for the price of a few days' entry. Passes are available to all visitors and prices were late increased in April 2019.

Discovery: €179	Magic Flex: €259	Magic Plus: €299	Infinity: €449
Access to the parks 150 days per year. Cannot be used 2nd and 3rd day after activation.	Access to the parks 300 days per year.	Access to the parks 350 days per year.	Access to the parks 365 days per year.
Unlimited parking add-on for €60.	Unlimited parking is included.	Unlimited parking is included.	Unlimited preferred parking is included.
	No shopping discount	Shops: 10% discount	Shops: 20% discount
	No dining discount	Dining: 10% discount	Dining: 15% discount
	Disney hotel rooms from €130 per night.	Disney hotel rooms from €130 per night.	Disney hotel rooms from €108 per night.
	20% off 1-day park entry tickets for family/friends	20% off 1-day park entry tickets for family/friends	20% off 1-day park entry tickets for family/friends
	1-Year PhotoPass add-on for €65	1-Year PhotoPass add-on for €59	1-Year PhotoPass package included
		20% off Buffalo Bills Wild West Dinner Show	20% off Buffalo Bills Wild West Dinner Show
		10% off Golf Disneyland and at French Disney Stores	10% off Golf Disneyland and at French Disney Stores
		Ten 1 day/2 park tickets each year for only €45 each.	Twenty 1 day/2 park tickets each year for only €39 each.
		Dedicated park entrances, access to Extra Magic Times & free non-alcoholic cocktail at Table Service Restaurants	Dedicated park entrances, access to Extra Magic Times, free locker, pushchair, kennel and wheelchair rentals and free non-alcoholic cocktail at Table Service Restaurants
			VIP viewing locations for *Disney Illuminations* and *Disney Stars on Parade* - reserve in advance.
			Dedicated phone line with concierge service.
			Access to pools at certain Disney hotels.

Annual Pass Blockout Dates

Discovery Pass:
July 2019 - *6 to 31*
August 2019 - *All month*
September 2019 - *Every Sat and Sun*
October 2019 - *5, 6, 12, 13, 19 to 31*
November 2019 - *1-3, 9-11, 16, 17, 23, 24 and 30*
December 2019 - *1, 7, 8, 14, 15, 21-31*
January 2020 - *1-5, 11, 12, 18, 19, 25 and 26*
February 2020 - *1, 2, 8-29*
March 2020 - *1-8, 14, 15, 21, 22, 28 and 29*
April 2020 - *4 to 30*
May 2020 - *1-3, 7-10, 16, 17, 21-24, 30 and 31*
June 2020 - *1, 6, 7, 13, 14, 20, 21, 27 and 28*
July 2020 - *4 to 31*
August 2020 - *All month*
September 2020 - *Every Sat and Sun*
October 2020 - *3, 4, 10, 11, 17, 18, 24-31*
November 2020 - *1-8, 11, 14, 15, 21, 22, 28 and 29*
December 2020 - *5, 6, 12, 13, 19-31*

Magic Flex Pass:
July 2019 - *None*
August 2019 - *14-16*
September 2019 - *None*
October 2019 - *19 to 31*
November 2019 - *1-3, 9-11 and 30*
December 2019 - *1, 7, 8, 14, 15, 21-31*
January 2020 - *1st only*
February 2020 - *15, 16, 22, 23 and 29*
March 2020 - *1st only*
April 2020 - *11, 12, 13, 18 and 19*
May 2020 - *1-3, 21-23, 30 and 31*
June 2020 - *1st only*
July 2020 - *None*
August 2020 - *14-16*
September 2020 - *None*
October 2020 - *24-31*
November 2020 - *1-2 and 11*
December 2020 - *5, 6, 19-31*

Magic Plus Pass:
July 2019 - *None*
August 2019 - *None*
September 2019 - *None*
October 2019 - *26 to 31*
November 2019 - *1 and 2*
December 2019 - *21 to 25*
January 2020 - *2nd only*
February 2020 - *None*
March 2020 - *None*
April 2020 - *None*
May 2020 - *None*
June 2020 - *None*
July 2020 - *None*
August 2020 - *None*
September 2020 - *None*
October 2020 - *28-31*
November 2020 - *1st only*
December 2020 - *26 to 31*

The Discovery pass can also NOT be used the two days following purchase.

Blackout dates are days when your pass does *not* allow you entry into the parks. They do not apply on the day you buy your annual pass, but you cannot park-hop on the day you purchase an annual pass if it is a blackout date. There is a 20% family discount if buying five annual passes together.

How do I get my annual pass?

At the ticket booths ask whether they can do an annual pass there and then - this is often available on quieter days of the week, and some weekends. Alternatively, ask if "Donald's Desk" is open. If so, follow the directions and complete the passport there.

If the desk is not open you will buy a one-day ticket to Disneyland Park (not Walt Disney Studios Park). Once inside Disneyland Park, visit the "Bureau Pass Annuel" (located at the entrance of Discoveryland).

Here you will be asked for some details such as your address and name, have a photo taken for the card and have your annual pass made. The price of your day ticket will be deducted from your annual pass' price.

Allow about an hour for this process, as there may be a wait – the actual process itself takes less than 10 minutes. You must take a passport or ID card with you as proof of identity.

TICKET TIPS

1. 2-Park tickets are called "Hoppers" as they allow you to go from one park to the other park as many times as you wish on the same day.
2. If you are visiting for three days or longer, consider getting an Annual Passport. It provides discounts on food, hotels, merchandise and more.

Understanding the Parks

Before taking a detailed look at each of the theme parks, we think it is best to explain some of the basics of each park, including parking, Fastpass, dining and much more.

Fastpass

Disneyland Paris offers a unique skip-the-queue system called Fastpass system *at no cost*. It allows you to reserve a time slot for certain attractions, return at an appointed time, and ride with little to no wait. While waiting for your Fastpass reservation time, you can do something else such as shop, dine, watch a show or experience another attraction.

HOW TO USE FASTPASS

❶ Find a Fastpass ride
You can identify rides that offer Fastpass by the *FP* logo on park maps. It is helpful to know which attractions offer Fastpass in advance by reading through this guide and looking at park maps.

❷ Check the wait time and decide
At a FP-enabled attraction, there are two ride entrances – the *standby* entrance where you can queue up and ride (e.g. 45-minute wait), and the *Fastpass* entrance.

If the standby wait time is short, use the regular standby entrance. If the wait is too long for you, then you should use the FP system. If the standby wait

is less than 30 minutes, we recommend waiting in the standby queue. This is because FPs often require you to backtrack across the park negating time savings.

❸ Get your Fastpass
Near the ride entrance is the FP distribution area with machines and a screen showing the current return time for FP reservations (e.g. 14:15 to 14:45). This is the time your reservation is made for and is printed on FPs.

Go to the FP machines and swipe or scan your park ticket or annual pass. The machine will print a paper FP telling you the time of your reservation. This is the same as that shown on the screen above the entrance.

Keep your FP and park ticket safe.

❹ Wait
Dine, explore the park or enjoy another ride or show until your FP return time.

❺ Return and Ride
Return to the ride during the time window on your FP, entering through the ride's Fastpass entrance. Hand your FP to the Cast Member at the Fastpass entrance who will keep it. Now, you can ride within a few minutes, skipping the regular queue – the wait time with a Fastpass is often under 5 minutes but can be up to 15 minutes.

THE FASTPASS SYSTEM EXPLAINED

Now that you have read about the advantages of the Fastpass system, we have to tell you the system's limitations - namely that you cannot use Fastpasses to avoid every single wait.

Firstly, not every ride offers Fastpass - only 10 rides out of 60 offer this service. Secondly, you can only hold one Fastpass ticket at a time, though there are exceptions to this as noted on the next page.

Therefore, you will likely use Fastpass throughout your time at Disneyland Paris but only occasionally.

How Fastpass works:
Every Disneyland Paris entry ticket and annual pass includes Fastpass access – it is a free system open to every guest.

Each day, Team Leaders will decide what percentage of riders they want to be able to use the Fastpass system. Let's say that in this case, it is 50%.

So, assuming 2000 guests per hour can ride *Big Thunder Mountain*, the Fastpass system will distribute 1000 Fastpass tickets for each operating hour. This means 50% of guests will use Fastpass to board, and 50% will use the standby queue each hour.

There are, therefore, a limited number of Fastpass tickets for each ride each hour. This is to ensure that the standby queue line is kept to a reasonable level.

The first Fastpass return time for an attraction is usually 30 minutes after park opening, although sometimes it is later.

Fastpass slots then move in 5-minute increments so after all the Fastpasses for 10:30am-11:00am are distributed, the next return time will be 10:35am-11:05am. Once all Fastpasses have been distributed for the day, the ticket distribution machines are shut down.

Rides may not offer Fastpasses for the entire park operating hours for operational reasons.

If you want to know the time of the last Fastpass return, ask the Cast Members at the attraction. When Fastpass stops being used, the regular queue usually moves twice as quickly.

Due to the limited number of Fastpasses available, tickets often run out on popular rides early in the day. This happens regularly on *Peter Pan's Flight, Big Thunder Mountain, Buzz Lightyear Laser Blast* and *Ratatouille: The Adventure*.

On busy days these rides will distribute their daily allocation of Fastpasses by lunchtime. *Ratatouille* regularly distributes all its Fastpass tickets within 30 minutes of the park opening.

Is Fastpass always available?
Most rides offer Fastpass daily. Others only offer Fastpasses when there are a certain number of guests in the park.

Rides that may not have Fastpasses available at off-peak times are: *Star Tours, Indiana Jones et le Temple du Peril, Rock 'n' Roller Coaster: Starring Aerosmith* and *Flying Carpets over Agrabah*.

Good to Know:
Tower of Terror and *Rock 'n' Roller Coaster* both have a compulsory pre-show video even in the Fastpass queue. After this, you enter a short queue line to board the ride vehicle itself, but the wait may be up to 15 minutes.

Buzz Lightyear, Star Wars Hyperspace Mountain and *Ratatouille* also often have a 15-minute wait before boarding with Fastpass.

On other attractions, you should be on the ride in less than five minutes after arriving with a Fastpass.

GET EXTRA FASTPASSES

Officially you can only hold one Fastpass at a time. However, there are exceptions.

• When your Fastpass return time begins, you can get another Fastpass even if you have not used your current Fastpass yet. E.g. You have a *Star Tours* Fastpass for 14:00-14:30. You can get another Fastpass from 14:00.

• Cast Members (at their discretion) may allow you to use a Fastpass after the return time, though not before. This is not allowed at *Ratatouille.*

• The Fastpass system is not connected between the two theme parks. Therefore, you can hold a Fastpass for a Walt Disney Studios Park ride and another for a Disneyland Park ride simultaneously.

Note that it can be a 20 to 30-minute walk from the back of one park to the other. You must have a 2-park 'hopper' ticket to enter both parks on the same day.

• If your return time is over two hours away, you can get a second Fastpass two hours after picking up the first. E.g. You got a *Star Wars Hyperspace Mountain* Fastpass at 10:00; the return time is 15:00-15:30. As 15:00 is over two hours away from when you got your Fastpass, you can get another Fastpass at 12:00 (two hours after 10:00). You can check the time your next Fastpass is available on the bottom of your latest Fastpass ticket.

• The *Indiana Jones* Fastpasses are not linked with the rest of the Fastpass system. This means you can hold a Fastpass for this attraction AND another Disneyland Park Fastpass at the same time.

FASTPASS ATTRACTIONS LIST

Disneyland Park:
• *Star Wars Hyperspace Mountain*
• *Buzz Lightyear Laser Blast*
• *Star Tours*
• *Peter Pan's Flight*
• *Indiana Jones et le Temple du Peril*
• *Big Thunder Mountain*

Walt Disney Studios Park:
• *The Twilight Zone: Tower of Terror*
• *Rock 'n' Roller Coaster: Starring Aerosmith*
• *Flying Carpets over Agrabah*
• *Ratatouille: The Adventure*

PREMIUM AND HOTEL FASTPASSES:

• Guests staying in suites at the Disneyland Hotel, Newport Bay Club Hotel, Hotel New York, Sequoia Lodge Hotel and Castle Club (Disneyland Hotel) receive one **VIP Fastpass** per guest. A VIP Fastpass offers instant, unlimited entry through the Fastpass line of every Fastpass attraction. With a VIP Fastpass, you do not need the regular Fastpass system. You show the VIP Fastpass at the entrance of each ride to access the Fastpass queue without a reservation. You must use standard queue lines at non-Fastpass attractions.

• Guests of the Golden Forest Club (Sequoia Lodge Hotel), Compass Club (Newport Bay Club Hotel) and Empire State Club (Hotel New York), are given one **Hotel Fastpass** per person per day. This allows guests to access one Fastpass attraction per day through the Fastpass queue instantly. The Hotel Fastpass is valid all day.

• Super Fastpass - This paid-for Fastpass grants access to either three family rides (Ratatouille, Peter Pan and Buzz Lightyear) or three thrill rides (Hyperspace Mountain, Rock 'n' Roller Coaster and Tower of Terror) one time each through the Fastpass queue line. Pricing is €30 per person in low season and €45 in high season.

• Ultimate Fastpass - This paid-for FastPass grants access to all Fastpass attractions. One entry to each attraction is priced at €60-€90 per person, whereas unlimited entries to all attractions is priced at €120-€150 per person, based on the season you visit.

On-Ride Photos

Some of Disneyland Paris' rides have cameras positioned and timed to take perfect on-ride photos of you at the most action filled moments on attractions. Buy the photo and see yourself at the fastest, steepest, scariest and most fun moment of the ride. These make for timeless keepsakes.

When you get off selected rides, you will walk past screens that preview your photo (with a watermark on top). If you wish to purchase it, go to the photo counter.

You do not have to buy on-ride photos straight after your ride; you can pick them up at any time that same day. Just remember your unique number at the ride exit or ask a member of staff at the photo kiosk to write it down for you.

If you like the photo, Cast Members will show it to you up close before you pay for it. If you like it, buy it! You will likely treasure the photo for a long time.

Photo print prices with frames are €20 for one photo, €26 for two photos and €36 for three photos. A single photo without a frame is €17, with each additional photo costing €10. Digital photos are also available via the Photopass+ app – more details on the following pages.

The attractions with on-ride photos are: *Big Thunder Mountain, Pirates of the Caribbean, Star Wars Hyperspace Mountain, Buzz Lightyear Laser Blast, Rock n' Roller Coaster* and *The Twilight Zone: Tower of Terror.*

Top Tip: If you want photos from several rides, you can combine these on a Photopass. See our section on Photopass to find out how to save money on photos.

Disneyland Paris App

Disneyland Paris has a free Apple iOS and Android app, which allows you to enhance your trip. With the app, you can plan your stay, including an overview of the hotels on offer, and a look at the different attractions throughout the resort. You can also create an itinerary.

Once in the park, you can check the opening hours, timings of shows and parades, and even the attraction wait times. It is this last feature that makes the app the most useful –

no more walking to the wait time board on Main Street, U.S.A. You can check waits in the palm of your hand for both parks at the same time.

You will need a data connection to see live information, which means you must have data roaming enabled on your phone.

Data usage is minimal for the app, but it may cost you depending on your roaming agreement if you are not from France.

Roaming charges within the EU have been abolished, meaning free roaming for EU residents.

Disneyland Paris plans to have free Wi-Fi available in both parks in the future.

Photopass

Disneyland Paris' Photopass is an easy to use system that makes collecting all your in-park photos easy.

Simply go to any in-park photographer (including those stationed at *Meet Mickey Mouse*, *Princess Pavilion*, and with other characters) and after your photo is taken, ask for a Disney Photopass.

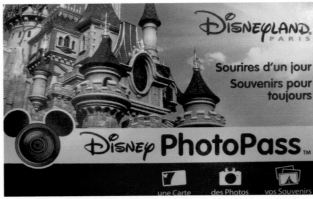

Alternatively, you can ask for a Photopass card at any ride photo counter (this option is not advertised, but it is available if you ask).

Next time you have a photo taken, hand over your card and pictures will be added onto it throughout your visit and be kept together on the system. This card can be re-used throughout both parks anywhere you find a photographer or with on-ride photos.

Photos are saved on the Photopass system for 7 days each.

Before your photos expire, visit one of these locations to view and purchase your photos: *New Century Notions: Flora's Unique*

Boutique in Disneyland Park, *Walt Disney Studios Store* in Walt Disney Studios Park, and *The Disney Gallery* in Disney Village. Photos can also be viewed at the Disney merchandise shops inside the on-site hotels.

At all these locations, you can purchase prints or digital versions of your Photopass photos. Multiple Photopass cards can be combined into one account too.

The more photos you purchase, the lower the overall 'price per photo' becomes.

You can also add an extra element of Disney magic with themed borders and details at no additional cost.

For those who have used Photopass in the American parks, the Disneyland Paris system works similarly, but the prints are generally more reasonably priced at Disneyland Paris.

The most significant difference, however, is the lack of Photopass photographers throughout the parks in France whereas there are many of them in each park in the US, allowing you to get great photos with the parks' icons. This is a photographer by Sleeping Beauty Castle and another on Town Square, but we hope this is expanded throughout the park in the future.

Photopass+

Like the regular Photopass (covered on the previous page), Photopass+ allows you to collect ride and character photos, as well as photos in front of some iconic park locations. The difference here is that you pre-pay for an unlimited number of digital photos instead of paying for each print individually. Photopass+ costs €75 at the park.

Photopass+ includes a Photopass+ card and a lanyard to carry the card on. In addition, two mini cards are included, so that other members of your party can have their own card and easily add photos to the same account. This allows groups and families to split up and get pictures added to the same account easily.

Guests can add an unlimited number of photos to their account for 10 days following their Photopass+ activation.

To view photos, guests should create an online account at disneyphotopass.eu or via the iOS and Android 'Disneyland Paris Photopass' mobile apps.

With the mobile app, after riding an attraction, you can scan a QR code on the ride photo preview monitors and add it to your account without needing to visit the ride photo counters. Guests can also type in the photo number as it appears on the photo preview screens. However, there are only Standard Definition photos - for High Definition photos you will need to ask a Cast Member at the purchase point.

Guests can view their photos on the DisneyPhotopass.eu website and download them in high quality, as well as buy prints, photo books, calendars, gifts and more.

Photos remain on the Photopass+ website for one year after they were taken, giving you time to download your favourite images.

Photopass+ at Disneyland Paris is very similar to the system in the US parks – but on a smaller scale.

Guests who pre-book Photopass+ as part of their stay pay €59. A Photopass+ voucher is given at check-in that must be exchanged for the actual product at any shop in the parks that sells Photopass+.

Top Tip: Annual Pass discounts are available. Annual pass holders also get a Photopass+ card valid for one year from the date of purchase instead of just 10 days, offering fantastic value for money.

Top Tip 2: If you have not bought Photopass+, you can also purchase individual digital photos on the Photopass app. These are £2.99/€3,59 each, or £7.99/€9,99 for six.

Top Tip 3: If you are only interested in ride photos from the five rides with on-ride cameras, then the PhotoPass+ Attractions One is ideal. The price is €40; the card can only be used to collect photos for one day.

Rider Switch

Rider Switch is a time-saving solution that allows parents to reduce queuing times throughout their visit when riding thrill attractions.

A common issue at theme parks is when two adults want to ride a thrill ride, but they have a child who is not tall enough to ride. There are three solutions:
a) the adults can take turns to ride (queuing twice);
b) one adult can choose not to experience the attraction;
c) skip the attraction.

The solution is Disney's Rider Switch, which allows one adult to queue up and ride while the other stays with the child.

When the first adult reaches the end of the queue line, they ask for a Rider Switch pass. The second adult is then able to ride as soon as the first one returns. The second adult is granted almost immediate access to the ride, usually through the exit, bypassing the entire regular queue line.

Each adult will experience the ride separately, but the second adult will not need to wait to ride.

Each attraction implements the system in a slightly different manner so ask Cast Members at ride entrances for details.

You do not need to have a child or baby present to use this service. You could use it to stay with an adult who does not wish to ride.

Single Rider

One of the best ways to significantly reduce your time waiting for attractions is to use the Single Rider queue instead of the regular standby queue. This is available at selected attractions at the resort.

The Single Rider queue fills free spaces on ride vehicles. For example, if a ride vehicle can seat 8 people and a group of 4 turns up, followed by a group of 3, then a Single Rider will fill the free space.

This allows guests who are willing to ride with strangers to experience a shorter wait, and fills a space. This system reduces waits for all.

Single Rider queues may be closed when waits in that queue are too long, or when the theme park is not busy.

Single Rider Lines can be used by groups too, but members of the group will be separated, and each will ride in a different vehicle. You can, of course, wait for

each other after riding by the exit but you will not ride together.

The following attractions operate Single Rider Lines:
• *RC Racer*
• *Toy Soldier Parachute Drop*
• *Crush's Coaster*
• *Ratatouille: The Adventure*
• *Star Wars Hyperspace Mountain*

Disneyland Paris wishes to increase the number of Single Rider lines at the parks in the future.

Larger Guests

Disneyland Paris has designed its attractions to be accessible to all guests, but sometimes a visitor's height or weight may limit the attractions they can visit for safety reasons.

At Disneyland Paris, unlike some other theme parks, there are no 'test seats' outside attractions. Therefore, if you are unsure

whether you will be able to ride a particular attraction, it is best to speak to a Cast Member at the ride entrance.

You could also ask the Cast Member whether they could allow you to try sitting in the ride vehicle itself before queuing up normally.

Rides where larger guests

may have difficulty include: *Rock 'n' Roller Coaster, Star Wars Hyperspace Mountain, Indiana Jones et le Temple du Peril, Crush's Coaster* and *RC Racer* because of the restraints and limited legroom.

Orbitron and *Cars Quatre Roues Rallye* may also be a tight fit despite using seatbelt-style restraints.

Extra Magic Time

Extra Magic Time (previously Extra Magic Hours) allow selected guests early theme park access to selected attractions at both theme parks at Disneyland Paris for over an hour each morning. Guests get access to an almost empty park, ride with little to no wait and can meet Disney characters too. EMT includes most of the major rides at both theme parks.

Extra Magic Times (EMT) take place at both theme parks daily from 8:30am to 9:30am. At selected times of the year, only one of the two theme parks may be open for EMT. Check the Disneyland Paris website for details.

Getting Extra Magic Time
The EMT benefit is available exclusively to guests staying at on-site Disney Hotels (not selected or partner hotel) and for guests who have a *Magic Plus* or *Infinity* Annual Passport, even if they are not staying at a Disney hotel.

Disney hotel guests will need their park tickets and their Magic Card or Easy Pass (given at hotel check-in) to gain entry during Extra Magic Time. Annual pass holders simply need their annual pass. Magic Plus Annual Pass holders may not enter during EMT on blackout dates.

What is open during EMT?
At Disneyland Park selected attractions on Main Street, U.S.A., Discoverland, Frontierland and Fantasyland.

Typically, the following rides are available during Extra Magic Time – other rides and lands open at the official park opening time: *Dumbo: The Flying Elephant, Peter Pan's Flight, Lancelot's Carousel, Mad Hatter's Teacups, Princess Pavilion, Meet Mickey Mouse, Buzz Lightyear Laser Blast, Star Tours, Hyperspace Mountain, Orbitron, Thunder Mesa Riverboat Landing and Big Thunder Mountain.*

Extra Magic Time at Walt Disney Studios Park includes the following attractions: *Crush's Coaster, RC Racer, Toy Soldiers Parachute Drop, Slinky Dog Zig Zag Spin, Flying Carpets Over Agrabah, The Twilight Zone: Tower of Terror, Rock 'n' Roller Coaster* and *Ratatouille: The Adventure.*

Wheelchair and Pushchair Rentals

Wheelchair and pushchair rentals are available for guests who do not wish to bring their own.

If your child is recently out of a pushchair, it is often still worth renting one as it is likely they will get tired, due to the larges walking distances involved with a Disneyland Paris visit.

Sometimes it is nice just to let kids sit in their pushchair and have a break. They can

also be used as an easy way to carry around bags.

It should be noted that Disneyland Paris' pushchairs do not recline, and do not have any real rain protection. Many guests also say that the pushchairs are not the most comfortable.

The daily cost of hiring a wheelchair or pushchair is €20. The deposit required for a wheelchair is €150; it is

€75 for a pushchair.

You are, of course, welcome to bring your own pushchair or wheelchair if you wish.

When experiencing attractions, be sure to leave your pushchair in the dedicated parking areas. Ask a Cast Member if you are not sure whether this is. Pushchairs may be moved by Cast Members to keep them neat and organised.

Guided Tours

If you want to discover more about the magic behind Disneyland Paris' two theme parks, be sure to join one of the resort's guided tours. Led by a Guest Relations Cast Member, these tours are the perfect way to enhance your visit.

The Disneyland Park tour (duration: 2 hours) departs at 1:00pm or 2:00pm daily, and the Walt Disney Studios Park tour (duration: 90 minutes) departs at 3:00pm each day.

You will discover the work that goes into creating these parks. You will find out secrets and notice details that will make you stop and say "wow".

The tour is available in the six official park languages, including English.

Additionally, *The Twilight Zone: Tower of Terror* tour goes into the details of the construction and design of The Hollywood Tower Hotel, as well as the references

from *The Twilight Zone* show.

The Tower of Terror Tour is held in French only at 9:10am on Wednesdays and Saturdays.

Pricing for the theme park tours is €65 per adult and €45 for children ages 3 to 11 inclusive. The *Tower of Terror* tour is €50 and €34.

Reservations can be made by emailing Disney Special Activities at dlp.disney. special.activities@disney.com.

Disney Shopping Service

The Disney Shopping Service allows you to buy an item at any of the theme park shops and pick it up later.

When paying for your goods before 3:00pm, ask to use the Disney Shopping Service. You will leave the item with the Cast Member who served you. When you have finished your day at the park, you can pick up your item.

You can then either pick up your purchases at the World

of Disney store in Disney Village in the evening, or at the Disney boutiques at on-site Disney hotels or selected partner hotels.

This means that you can collect all your items in one spot, even if you have multiple items from different shops.

This service allows you to be free to eat, shop, ride attractions and watch shows to your heart's content without carrying any bags.

Lockers

There are two staffed luggage services located to the right of the entrances to the theme parks.

There is also an external automatic left luggage storage facility on the upper level of *Marne-La-Vallee – Chessy* rail station.

Lockers at the parks and in the station range in price from €5 to €10 depending

on the size of the locker and number of bags stored.

For the station lockers, you need exact change (there is a change machine inside the locker room). At the Disney Parks, you can pay by cash or by card.

Infinity Annual Pass holders may store one item per day at the parks at no cost.

You can access the Disneyland Paris park lockers as many times as you want throughout the day for one set daily fee. With the station lockers, every time you open the lockers, you must pay again to lock them. Plus, you must go back and forth through Disneyland Paris security checkpoint each time to access the station lockers.

Meeting the Disney Characters

For many visitors, meeting characters is the highlight of their trip. Playing with Pluto, talking to Cinderella and hugging Mickey makes for magical memories.

Disneyland Park:
Characters are scheduled to appear around the park throughout the day.

Mickey is at *Meet Mickey Mouse* in Fantasyland, and the Disney princesses can be found at *Princess Pavilion* (also in Fantasyland).

Near *Alice's Curious Labyrinth*, you will find Alice and her friends, including The Mad Hatter and Tweedle Dum and Dee. Also nearby, you can meet Winnie the Pooh and Friends.

By Casey's Corner you can see Donald and friends, whereas by the *Liberty Arcade*, you can find Minnie and friends.

Woody and Friends are by Cowboy Cookout Restaurant, Baloo can be found by Hakuna Matata Restaurant in Adventureland and Chip and Dale are near Colonel Hathi's Pizza Outpost.

Elsewhere in Adventureland, you can expect to see Peter Pan and friends by *Pirate's Beach*, and Aladdin and friends near Agrabah Café.

At Starport in Discoveryland, you can meet Darth Vader.

If there is a specific character you would like to see, ask at City Hall (on Town Square) whether they have a schedule for them. Not all characters are available to meet daily.

You can also have a Disney

princess dining experience at *L'Auberge de Cendrillon* (€77 per adult, €45 per child).

You are also able to meet Disney characters at Plaza Gardens on Main Street, U.S.A for breakfast.

Characters usually stop meeting in both parks by mid-afternoon. Check the in-park schedule for details.

Walt Disney Studios Park:
You will find many characters in the Toon Studio area of the park to the left of *Crush's Coaster* at permanent outdoor photo locations. Here you will often find Mickey, Minnie, Buzz Lightyear, Woody and other characters. Check your Times Guide for exact character appearances.

For some characters at the Studios Park, instead of queuing up to meet, you must download an app called 'Lineberty' and 15 minutes before the character is set to meet, book a free reservation.

Guests can meet and greet

Spider-Man at *Meet Spider-Man*, located just opposite *Rock 'n' Roller Coaster*. Other Marvel characters may replace Spider-Man at this location in the future.

Hotels:
Characters are present at on-site hotels in the morning.

Classic characters such as Mickey, Minnie, Tigger, Chip and Dale and Donald Duck are also present during the character meals at Inventions restaurant in the Disneyland Hotel. Lunch and Dinner meals are priced at €69 adults, and €39 for kids. Inventions also hosts a themed brunch on Sundays priced at €99 adults, €45 kids, from 1:00pm to 3:00pm – you can book both even if you are not staying here.

Disney Village:
At *Buffalo Bill's Wild West Show* you can get a photo with Mickey in his Wild West costume before the show. Be there early as Mickey heads off early to prepare for the show. Show admission tickets are required.

How to Spend Less Time Queuing

Disneyland Paris meticulously themes its queues to introduce an attraction's story before you board. However, no one likes waiting, and often you want to ride as quickly as possible. Remember that a visit to a theme park will involve waiting in queue lines; this chapter covers our top tips on minimising these waits.

❶ Eat outside the regular dining hours

At Disneyland Paris, whether you want to eat at a Table Service restaurant or a Quick Service meal, waiting for your food is part of the game. Have lunch before midday or after 3:00pm for much shorter waits. In addition, having dinner before 7:00pm will reduce your time waiting. A wait of 45 minutes or longer just to order is relatively typical at peak times at Quick Service restaurants.

❷ Quick Service meal tricks

At Quick Service locations, cashiers have two queues, and alternate between them – count how many groups (families) are in front of you in the queue. There may be ten people in front of you in one queue line but only two families. The other queue line may have five people but from five different families. The queue with ten people will move more quickly with only two orders to process versus the other queue's five orders.

❸ On-site Disney hotel guests

If you are staying at an on-site Disneyland Paris hotel, take advantage of Extra Magic Times. You get entry into both theme parks over one hour before regular guests do. During this time, you can experience many of the park's attractions with minimal waits. See our Extra Magic Times section for more details.

❹ Disneyland Park opens early

Disneyland Park's opening hours usually state it officially opens at 10:00am, but guests can enter the park 30 minutes earlier. This means you can enter the park, enjoy the atmosphere, eat breakfast, start shopping and take photos of Main Street, U.S.A. and Sleeping Beauty Castle. In front of the castle, the entrances to all the lands will be cordoned off by Cast Members.

If you are a Disney hotel guest or a Magic Plus or Infinity annual pass holder, show your Magic Card or annual pass, and you can enter Fantasyland, Discoveryland and Frontierland. Otherwise, wait by the ropes at the entrances of the lands for "rope-drop" as the park opens. If you are there before the park opens, you can be on your first ride in minutes.

❺ Walt Disney Studios Park opens early

Walt Disney Studios Park also opens at 9:30am. At that time, you can walk around the entire park, and most attractions will be operational due to Extra Magic Time having started an hour earlier. Some attractions will only open at 10:00am at the official park opening time. We recommend going straight to ride *Crush's Coaster*.

❻ Crush's Coaster does not have Fastpass

If you plan on experiencing *Crush's Coaster*, we cannot overstate how important it is for you to be at Walt Disney Studios Park's turnstiles before 9:30am. By doing this you will be able to go through the turnstiles when the park pre-opens and make your way to *Crush's Coaster*. Note that due to selected guests having access with Extra Magic Times there may already be a wait for this ride at regular park opening, but this will likely be the shortest wait for this ride of the whole day. See 'Chapter 10: Touring Plans' for more details on how to maximise your time at the park. Alternatively, use the Single Rider queue line to save a lot of time.

❼ Skip the parades and fireworks

If you have already seen the parades, shows or fireworks, use that time to experience rides as the wait times are often much shorter during these big events. If you have not seen the park's entertainment offerings before, we do not recommend you skip them. Parades and shows are only performed at set times of the day and most of these are as good as, if not better, than many rides.

❽ Ride outdoor attractions when it rains

Outdoor attractions such as *Dumbo, Flying Carpets over Agrabah, Casey Junior, Storybook Canal boats, Big Thunder Mountain, Indiana Jones et le Temple du Peril, Lancelot's Carousel* (outdoor queue), *Slinky Dog Zigzag Spin, Toy Soldiers Parachute Drop* and *RC Racer* have significantly reduced waits when it is raining. Yes, you may get soaked while riding (a jacket may help) but the wait times will be shorter.

Top Tip: Many guests return to the hotels when it rains, so many of the indoor rides may also have shorter queues during inclement weather.

❾ Choose when to visit carefully

Visit during an off-peak time if possible. If you are visiting on New Year's Day, expect to queue a lot longer than in the middle of February. Of course, weekends are busier than weekdays. See our 'When to Visit' section to make the most of your time.

❿ Shop at the start or end of the day

If you enter the park during the pre-opening period from 9:30am to 10:00am, this is a perfect time to go shopping. Alternatively, go shopping at the end of the day. Even when the park is 'officially' closed, the shops on Main Street, U.S.A. stay open up to an hour longer than the rest of the park. Alternatively, walk over to Disney Village in the evening, and go shopping there until midnight or 1:00am on most days!

Additionally, on-site hotels and some partner hotels have a small Disney boutique inside them. Do not waste your time during the day shopping, do it at strategic times and make the most of your time in the parks.

⓫ Get a Times Guide

Get your Park Map and the Times Guide on the way in; you will usually find them distributed together. The Times Guide lists all time-sensitive information at the parks such as the timings of parades, shows, character appearances and more. As such, you will not waste time crossing the park to find out that a character you saw earlier in the day has now left a particular location.

Dining

There are a variety of places to eat at Disneyland Paris. Food options vary from sandwich and snack locations to Quick Service (fast food) places, character buffets, Table Service dining and even fine dining options. Eating can be as much a part of the experience as the attractions at Disneyland Paris.

Making Reservations

If you want to guarantee you will be able to dine at a specific restaurant, it is worth booking a table in advance.

You can make your restaurant reservation up to 60 days in advance, but in reality, booking even two weeks or less beforehand will usually get you a table at most places.

Most people do not book restaurants in theme parks in Europe far in advance, which is a stark change from the American Disney parks.

Despite this, it is worth making a reservation as early as possible if you want a meal on a specific day. You will also be seated much more quickly with a reservation than without

one.

Purchasing a meal plan does not guarantee you a table in a restaurant, so be sure to make a restaurant reservation in advance if there is a particular place you want to dine.

You can call the Dining Reservation hotline on +33 (0)1 60 30 40 50 and book in several languages, including English. You can also book at City Hall in Disneyland Park, Studio Services in Walt Disney Studios or at any of the Disney hotel lobbies. In addition, you can visit any of the restaurants and book directly.

You do not need to be staying in a Disney hotel to book a table at a restaurant. If you cannot attend a

reservation, it is good practice to cancel it as soon as possible.

In low season, it is possible to make reservations for the same day or the next day. In the high season, restaurants are fully booked a week or more in advance.

Top Tip: If you wish to dine at Auberge de Cendrillon, specifically, it is worth booking as soon as reservations open - it is very popular.

Online Reservations: At the time of writing, Disneyland Paris is trialing online dining reservations. Visit fan website Salon Mickey for direct links to each restaurant's reservation page. Visit tiny.cc/dlpdining.

Meal Plans

Meal Plans allow you to pre-purchase meal credits so that on arrival at the resort, you do not need to worry about the cost of meals. Meal Plans are available to guests who book packages with an official Disney hotel and park tickets.

A meal voucher includes a set menu or buffet, and one soft drink.

Occasionally, Disneyland Paris runs a promotion with a free Meal Plan included with package bookings.

Meal plan entitlements are digitally loaded onto your Magic Card which is given upon check-in at the hotel. In some cases, including if using the Disney Express service, you may be given paper vouchers instead.

There are three different Meal Plans from which to choose. More expensive Meal Plans include pricier restaurants and food items.

Not every restaurant accepts every Meal Plan; if you eat at a restaurant which is not included on your Meal Plan, you can use your vouchers for a discount. E.g. If you a have a 'Plus' voucher, but visit a 'Premium' restaurant, the 'Plus' voucher's value is deducted from your bill, and you pay the difference.

Vouchers are valid at most Quick Service locations. We do not recommend this as the vouchers are worth more than a Quick Service meal so you would be wasting their value.

Meal Plans can save you up to 15% off the meal prices, although this varies based on what you eat. For many guests, the peace of mind of pre-paid meals is the best part.

Meals are from a set menu on the "Standard" and "Plus" plans. On the Premium Plan you can order 'a la carte'. If in doubt, ask your waiter before ordering.

The Half Board plan includes one voucher for any restaurant from the grid on the next page; the Full Board plan includes two vouchers for restaurants of your choice from the grid. Breakfast is also included.

Pricing:
When booking, you can either choose a Half Board option breakfast plus one meal per day, or a Full Board option for breakfast plus two meals per day. Prices are below and are per night of a stay - breakfast is an extra charge for guests without meal plans.

	Standard Adult	Standard Child	Plus Adult	Plus Child	Premium Adult	Premium Child
Half Board	€39	€28	€55	€38	€89	€62
Full Board	€59	€42	€75	€52	€120	€81

Restaurant Name	Restaurant Type	Location	On Standard Plan?	On Plus Plan?	On Premium Plan?
Agrabah Cafe	Buffet	Disneyland Park	Yes	Yes	Yes
Annette's Diner	Table Service	Disney Village	No	Yes	Yes
Auberge de Cendrillon	Table Service	Disneyland Park	No	No	Yes
Beaver Creek Tavern	Table Service	Sequoia Lodge Hotel	No	Yes	Yes
Bistrot Chez Remy	Table Service	Walt Disney Studios Park	No	Yes	Yes
Buffalo Bill's Wild West Show	Table Service Show	Disney Village	No	No	Yes
Cafe Mickey	Table Service	Disney Village	No	Yes	Yes
California Grill	Table Service	Disneyland Hotel	No	No	Yes
Cape Cod	Buffet	Newport Bay Club Hotel	No	Yes	Yes
Captain Jack's	Table Service	Disneyland Park	No	Yes	Yes
Chuck Wagon Cafe	Buffet	Hotel Cheyenne	Yes	Yes	Yes
Crockett's Tavern	Buffet	Davy Crockett's Ranch	Yes	Yes	Yes
Hunter's Grill	Buffet	Sequoia Lodge Hotel	No	Yes	Yes
Inventions	Character Buffet	Disneyland Hotel	No	No	Yes
La Cantina	Buffet	Santa Fe Hotel	Yes	Yes	Yes
La Grange at Billy Bob's	Table Service	Disney Village	Yes	Yes	Yes
Manhattan Restaurant	Table Service	Hotel New York	No	Yes	Yes
Plaza Gardens	Buffet	Disneyland Park	Yes	Yes	Yes
Parkside Diner	Buffet	Hotel New York	No	Yes	Yes
Restaurant des Stars	Buffet	Walt Disney Studios Park	Yes	Yes	Yes
Silver Spur Steakhouse	Table Service	Disneyland Park	No	Yes	Yes
The Steakhouse	Table Service	Disney Village	No	Yes	Yes
Walt's: An American Restaurant	Table Service	Disneyland Park	No	No	Yes
Yacht Club	Table Service	Newport Bay Club Hotel	No	Yes	Yes

Tipping in Restaurants

In France, a 15% service charge is included in your meal price, although this may not be itemised in the bill.

You are not expected to leave any additional money for service.

If you particularly liked the service, free to leave a few Euros in cash as a tip. A 5% to 10% tip is more than enough, although French guests rarely leave a tip.

Sometimes in France, waiters will not return with your change and will assume it is their tip; if this was not your intention, make this known. This is much less common at Disneyland Paris than elsewhere. One way to avoid this is to always pay by card.

Good to Know

• For buffets, kids' prices apply for those aged 3 to 11.

• You have the option of breakfast at Plaza Gardens in Disneyland Park for €25 per person. Ask at reception for the availability of this experience if you do not book in advance.

• Adults can order from the kids' menu at Quick Service locations. At Table Service locations, this is at the discretion of the Cast Member serving you.

• For an idea of how much food costs at the restaurants, see our parks chapters which list set menu prices and a la carte main courses.

• Not all restaurants have a vegan or vegetarian option, but Cast Members and chefs will do their best to accommodate you. Making a reservation and stating your dietary requirements helps.

Breakfast Pricing

Breakfast is not included with hotel reservations. Unless you purchase a meal plan, you will need to pay for breakfast separately.

These are the breakfast prices per person per night:
• **Davy Crockett Ranch** - €10 adult or child
• **Santa Fe & Cheyenne** - €19 per adult, €14 per child
• **Sequoia Lodge** - €19 per adult, €17 per child
• **Newport Bay Club & Hotel New York** - €25 per adult, €23 per child
• **Disneyland Hotel** - €30 per adult, €27 per child

To eat breakfast in the park with Disney characters, the full price is €35 per person - guests with one of the above meal plans, simply pay the difference.

RESTAURANT TYPES:

Buffet – All-you-can-eat locations where you fill your plate from the food selection as many times as you want. Buffets may or may not include drinks.

Quick Service – Fast food. Look at the menus, pay for your food and collect it a few minutes later. You will find everything from burgers and chips, to chicken, to pizza and pasta. Be aware that Disney 'fast'-food locations are notoriously slow and a queue of just four or five people in front of you can easily be a wait time of 20 to 30 minutes.

Table Service – Where you order from a menu, and are served by a waiter who brings your food to your table.

Character Buffets – These are available all day and are all-you-can-eat places where characters interact with you and take photos as you eat.

Top Tip: Whether it be a snack cart, a Quick Service location or a Table Service restaurant, you are never obliged to order from a set menu. Ordering specific items 'a la carte' is completely fine, although it may save you money if you order certain set menu combinations.

Disneyland Park

The first park at Disneyland Paris is composed of five lands filled with fantasy, adventure and excitement.

Disneyland Park, also known as *Parc Disneyland* in French, is based on the original Disneyland that opened in California in 1955. Every Disney resort around the world has one of these classic "Magic Kingdom-style" Disney parks. The park spans 140 acres, which is almost twice the size of the original.

Disneyland Park is the most visited theme park in Europe and the thirteenth most visited in the world, with 9.8 million visitors in 2019. The park has plenty to offer guests with almost fifty attractions (rides, themed areas and shows), as well as character experiences, dining options and plenty of places to shop.

Disneyland Park is, in our opinion, easily the best theme park in Europe, and it is commonly heralded as the most beautiful Disney theme park in the world.

The park is divided into five areas (or "lands") around Sleeping Beauty Castle in the centre. These are Main Street USA, Frontierland, Adventureland, Fantasyland and Discoveryland. Each land has its own overarching theme, with its own soundtrack, décor, costumes and themed attractions. Around the edges of the park, you will find the Disneyland Railroad, which transports guests between these different lands.

We will now take a look at each land individually, as well as their attractions, dining options and other notable features.

As queuing is inevitable at theme parks, in order to help you determine how long you may wait to experience the attractions, we have included "average wait times"; these are for peak times such as school holidays (Summer, Christmas, Easter) and weekends throughout the year. Wait times outside busy times are often lower.

ATTRACTION KEY:
In the sections that follow, the following symbols are used when describing attractions.

 Fastpass?   On-Ride Photo?   Average Wait Time

Minimum Height   Ride Length

Main Street, U.S.A.

Main Street, U.S.A. is the entrance to Disneyland Park, taking you towards Sleeping Beauty Castle and beyond.

Main Street, U.S.A. is the entrance area of Disneyland Park, leading you towards Sleeping Beauty Castle. This area of the park is themed to look like 1920s America.

It contains many shops on both sides of the street, the king of which is the **Emporium** where you are sure to find something to buy!

There are places to eat up and down the street too, including Quick Service and Table Service restaurants, as well as snack locations. There are also other food shops and carts around Main Street, U.S.A. too.

Before entering Main Street, U.S.A. itself, there is Town Square with a gazebo in the centre.

City Hall is immediately to your left on Town Square; this is "Guest Services". Ask any questions you have here. They can also make reservations for tours and restaurants, and accept complaints and positive feedback too.

For disabled guests, an accessibility card is available at City Hall providing easier access to attractions. See our 'Guests with Disabilities' section for more information on this.

Running parallel to Main Street, U.S.A. are the **Liberty Arcade** and **Discovery Arcade**. These provide an alternative route through the park when it is raining.

The Disney Imagineers

learnt a valuable lesson from the other Disney theme parks, where Main Street, U.S.A. became congested during parades, shows and at the end of the day. The arcades allow an alternative route to Main Street, U.S.A., making the guest experience better.

You will often find character meet and greets in this area of the park, as well as live music.

Top Tip: As you walk up Main Street, U.S.A. listen to the sounds from the windows on the first floor to hear the noise that the town's residents make. You can hear a dentist in one window, a man taking a bath in another and even a piano recital!

Attractions

Disneyland Railroad - Main Street, U.S.A. Station

Take a grand tour of Disneyland Park onboard an authentic steam train. Whether you use it as a form of transportation or just a way of seeing the sights, the Disneyland Railroad is a fun way to enjoy the park.

A full trip around the park takes 20 to 30 minutes.

This attraction usually ceases operation several hours before the park closes.

Main Street Vehicles and Horse-Drawn Streetcars

What better way to see Main Street, U.S.A. than from a vehicle – whether it is a horse-drawn car, a double decker bus or one of the other forms of transport.

These vehicles typically only operate in the morning, and you simply wait for the next vehicle to turn up at designated spots.

Throughout the day, at unannounced times, the fountains in the moat of Sleeping Beauty Castle come to life, along with music, for special two to three minute happenings.

This takes place eight times per day but no schedule is officially published. If you are there on the hour or at half-past the hour, you are more likely to see these.

These fountain shows change according to the seasons, with seasonal variations during Halloween, Christmas and St. Patrick's Day, for example.

DINING

Walt's Restaurant – Table Service. There are three different set menus priced from €41 to €70. Some menu items are included in the Premium Meal Plan. A la carte mains are priced between €40 and €50. A vegan set menu is available.

Casey's Corner – Counter Service. Serves ballgame themed snacks. Classic hot dogs - €8.50; 8-piece chicken nuggets - €8; salad - €7; desserts - €2 to €4; hot and cold drinks - €3.30 to €3.70; brownie and hot drink deal - €5.60; beer - €5.90). Cheddar and onions can be added for a few €0.50 more to the hot dog.

Plaza Gardens – Buffet. Adult buffet priced at €35 with drinks. Child buffet priced at €18 with one drink. Both adult and child buffets are included in the Standard Meal Plan. A character breakfast is available here for €35 per person.

Victoria's Home-Style Restaurant – Counter Service. Hot sandwiches - €7; side salad - €3.50; crisps - €2.30; desserts - €3 to €4; hot and cold drinks €2.80 to €3.50; teatime treat - €5.60; beer - €5.40. Serves milkshakes in warmer months.

Frontierland

Step into Frontierland and be transported to the Wild Western town of Thunder Mesa.

Attractions

In addition to the attractions featured on the following pages, you may also wish to visit **Rustler Roundup Shootin' Gallery** where you can practice your shooting skills in a carnival-style game. There is an additional charge for this attraction.

Other attractions in this land include the **Frontierland Railroad Station**, the **Keelboats** which have been closed for several years, and **Pocahontas Indian Village** - a themed outdoor playground. Finally, at the **Frontierland Theater** you can take in a seasonal live show: in the past these have included Lion King, Frozen and Forest of Enchantment.

Big Thunder Mountain

| Yes | 1.02m | Yes | 4 minutes | 90 to 120 minutes |

According to Disney legend, Big Thunder Mountain and the town of Thunder Mesa were discovered in the late 1800s.

In the town, a train line was constructed to transport ore around the mountain. However, the town was cursed, and it was subsequently struck by an earthquake.

Residents left the town, but a few years later the trains were found driving themselves around the mountain.

Guests can now take a 4-minute ride in one of these mine trains for themselves.

Along the way, you will see collapsing bridges, experience a dynamite blast, see bats and feel much more on this wild ride!

Most of the action takes place on an island in the middle of the lake, making it a unique version of the ride when compared to other Disney parks.

It is also the longest, tallest and fastest of the Big Thunder Mountain rides around the world but is by far the most family-friendly of the resort's roller coasters.

At the end, you can also purchase your on-ride photo if you wish.

This is one of our favourite attractions in the park and should not be missed.

Phantom Manor

| FP | No | | None | 📷 | No | ⌄ | 7 minutes | ⧗ | Less than 30 minutes |

Phantom Manor has a dark storyline: on her wedding day, Melanie eagerly awaited her groom, not knowing that a phantom haunted the house she was in. The phantom (Melanie's father) lured the groom into the attic and hanged him. Melanie waited for her groom, but he never turned up. Now, she roams around the manor still in her wedding dress. Today, you venture through this derelict manor as you discover Melanie's story.

Phantom Manor is a must-see attraction: the atmosphere, music and details are amongst the best in the whole resort.

The storyline of this attraction is unique, despite similar rides existing at other Disney parks worldwide.

After a walk-through section featuring the manor's lobby and other rooms, guests sit in "doombuggies" for the ride portion of the attraction. These rotate and tilt to show guests parts of the mansion as they travel through it.

You can expect to see pianos playing by themselves, door knockers that have a mind of their own, a seance, and ghosts gathering for a ballroom dance.

Throughout the attraction, there are no jump-out scares, but the initial walk-through section may frighten some children due to the effects used here, and the dark. The animatronics in the cemetery scene may also frighten young children. These do pass by relatively quickly.

Phantom Manor is not a horror-maze attraction with actors jumping out to scare you, and as there is no height restriction, the attraction is accessible to all ages. However, do be wary with younger kids.

If you are unsure whether your child will be comfortable with the ride, try doing it during the daytime when the building's exterior looks less imposing. You could also try watching an on-ride video online before your visit.

Also, we recommend not making this your first ride as we have heard many stories of children riding Phantom Manor at the start of a trip and then refusing to go on any other rides as they are scared.

We highly recommend making a stop at this ride as it is a true Disney classic, and as Melanie says: "Be sure to bring your death certificate. We're just *dying* to have you."

Thunder Mesa Riverboat Landing

Set sail on a classic riverboat around Big Thunder Mountain and admire Frontierland's landscape.

The Thunder Mesa Riverboat is a relaxing change of pace from the crowds in the park and there is plenty of space to roam around the boat.

There are some (limited) seating areas and you can listen to the story of the Molly Brown riverboat as you go around the river via the speakers, though the audio is not particularly loud - most people just take

No	None	No	15 mins	Less than 30 mins

in the atmosphere.

Top Tip: The Riverboat's operating hours are shorter than most other attractions. It often closes in the middle of the afternoon or early evening.

THERE'S MORE TO FRONTIERLAND THAN MEETS THE EYE

As well as the major attractions featured on these pages, you should also enjoy the little details that make Frontierland unique. As you walk into Frontierland from Central Plaza, stop by **Fort Comstock**, the timber-themed entrance to the land. Notice the little details here, and if the steps are open on the left, climb up for a different perspective on this area.

Phantom Manor has its own cemetery at the exit called **Boot Hill**. When you come out of the attraction, you can either turn right down the hill to the front of the manor or continue straight ahead to Boot Hill. This area contains tombstones of several Thunder Mesa residents, which all tell their own story through gags and rhymes. You can also access Boot Hill if you are not riding Phantom Manor by walking up the hill to the right of the house.

Even the restaurants and shops are filled with details. Inside, **The Lucky Nugget Saloon** is a stage where live music and other acts perform. **Cowboy Cookout BBQ** also has live music, and the Imagineers went to town with the theming. Notice the chairs, for example - unlike other restaurants where everything is uniform, here there are many different types and styles of chairs because in the Wild West the townsfolk would bring chairs from home.

DINING

Silver Spur Steakhouse – Table Service. The 2-course Sheriff menu is €30, and the 3-course Sheriff menu is €37 - both without drinks. A 3-course Cowboy menu is €43. Main courses are €22 to €40 a la carte. The children's menu is €18 with one drink and €32 for the premium menu. The children's set menu and 3-course Sheriff menu are on the Plus Meal Plan. The kid's Premium Menu is on the Premium Meal Plan.

The Lucky Nugget Saloon – Counter Service. Set menus are priced at €22 for an adult, and €13 for a child. A la carte main courses are €15 to €17.

Cowboy Cookout Barbecue – Counter Service. Set menus are priced at €14 to €17 for adults and €9 for children. A la carte main courses are €7 to €13.

Fuente del Oro – Counter Service serving Mexican fare. Set menus are priced at €13 to €17. The children's menu is priced at €9. A la carte main courses are €7.50 to €13.

Last Chance Cafe – Counter Service. Take-away snack meals such as vegan chilli 'con carne' and chicken wings are €7 to €8. Desserts, beer, and hot and cold drinks are also available.

Adventureland

Venture into an Arabian story, the Caribbean or a temple with Indiana Jones.

Attractions

In addition to the attractions covered below, you may also want to check out **Adventure Isle** (a walkthrough area with winding paths, caves, a pirate ship and a suspension bridge), **Le Passage Enchante d'Aladdin** (a walkthrough attraction depicting scenes from the story of Aladdin) and **La Plage des Pirates** (an outdoor playground).

Indiana Jones et le Temple du Peril:

| Yes | 1.40m | No | 2 minutes | 30 to 60 minutes |

This roller coaster will take you on an archaeological adventure through the lost Temple of Doom.

Your adventure will have you climbing in search of treasure, dropping and turning around tight corners, and meandering in and around the Temple. You will even descend rapidly into a 360-degree loop as your mine cart goes out of control.

The ride has the biggest minimum-height limit of any ride at any Disney park worldwide – 140cm. It was also the first Disney roller coaster in the world to go upside down. The ride even ran backwards for a few years, but now runs forward once again.

This is one of the most intense coasters at the resort with the loop being particularly tight. It is also quite a rough ride.

Of all the coasters in the park, this ride usually has the shortest queue as it is hidden at the back of the park, and the big minimum height means it is off-limits to most kids under the age of 10.

Overall, it is a relatively short but fun experience.

Top Tip: When park attendance is low, Fastpass is not offered at this attraction.

Top Tip 2: Although this attraction does sometimes get long wait times, it is almost always deserted after the daily parade.

Pirates of the Caribbean

FP No	None	Yes	10 minutes	15 to 45 minutes

Ahoy me hearties! Set sail through the world of the Pirates of the Caribbean at Disneyland Paris.

Board a boat and enjoy a ten-minute journey into a fort invaded by pirates.

Your boat will ascend and go down two short flume drops. You are unlikely to get wet, but it may happen.

The audio-animatronic characters in the attraction are enthralling, and it may just be the best-themed attraction in all of Disneyland Park. The attention to detail is fantastic, from the queue line to the Cast Members' costumes and the music to the sets.

This attraction is based on the original Pirates of the Caribbean ride in Disneyland in California.

Pirates of the Caribbean was the final ride Walt Disney himself supervised the creation of at Disneyland.

In 2017, the ride went through a huge update with new additions, so keep your eyes peeled for some well-known film characters including Jack Sparrow, Blackbeard and Barbossa.

Be aware that the queue line for the ride is not well lit due to the atmosphere it aims to create, and therefore it is very dark. This will especially strike you during the daytime when your eyes take a while to adjust, so we would advise holding onto your children's hands throughout the queue line.

This ride's loading system is very efficient, and it has the highest capacity in the park, but it is also an extremely popular ride. This means that although most of the year waits stay below 20 minutes, on peak days, you may see these rise to 60 minutes. The queue line is almost always moving, and once you are in the indoor section, there is a lot to see.

The recommended minimum age for this attraction is 12 months old as it is dark and loud.

This a must-see, family-friendly ride that is a classic Disney experience.

Warning: As the queue line for this attraction is so dark and there are so many people in one place, it is a favourite spot for pickpockets – especially when there are long waits. Be aware of your surroundings and keep an eye on your belongings.

La Cabane des Robinson

No	None	No	5 minutes	None - walkthrough

Enter the world of Swiss Family Robinson as you explore the treehouse made from the wood of their shipwreck. You can see the complex water wheel system they built to get water up to the bedrooms, and explore the kitchen, living rooms and bedrooms. This is a walkthrough experience and kids generally enjoy exploring and climbing the steps.

From the top, the view is mostly obscured by the tree's leaves, but you can get an interesting perspective on the park from up here.

ADVENTURELAND IS DESIGNED TO BE EXPLORED ON FOOT...

Of all the lands at Disneyland Park, Adventureland is the one that appears to have the smallest number of attractions. However, this area of the park is filled with incredible details that you need to find for yourself outside of the main attractions. Adventureland is built around Adventure Isle, with La Cabane des Robinson at the centre. As well as the treehouse, be sure to step aboard the **Pirate Galleon** moored in the centre of the land, and explore the caves under the treehouse to see the secrets that lie here. There are also a separate set of **caves** next to the galleon - here you will find treasure, skeletons and cascading waterfalls. Be sure to follow the signs to "Pont Suspendu" to reach **Spyglass Hill** and enjoy the stunning view over the park. Don't forget to cross the wobbly **Suspension Bridge** and the **Floating Bridge** ("Pont Flotant") which is located next to the Swiss Family Robinson's shipwreck.

DINING

Captain Jack's – Table Service. Adult set menus are priced between €40 and €56. The children's set menu is priced at €19, with a premium kids' menu priced at €33. Select menus are on the Plus Meal Plans - you can order any item a la carte with the Premium Meal Plan.
Agrabah Cafe – Buffet. The adult buffet is €35 with one drink. The children's buffet is €18 with one drink. The child and adult buffets are included in the Standard Meal Plan.
Colonel Hathi's Pizza Outpost – Counter Service. Set menus are priced between €14 and €16. The children's set menu is priced at €9.
Hakuna Matata – Counter Service. Set menus are priced at €13 to €15. The children's set menu is priced at €9. Serves pizzas, pastas and salads.
Coolpost – Snacks. Hot dogs - €7.50; teatime drink and donut - €5.60; ice creams - €3 to €4; and crepes - €3 to €4. Other small snacks, as well as hot and cold drinks are sold.

Fantasyland

Find classic Disney attractions here, in this land dedicated to the youngest members of the family.

Attractions

Disneyland Park's gentle toddler-friendly rides are found here in the most magical of all the lands, and there is plenty of variety. In addition to the attractions covered in depth on the following pages, you may also want to visit **Sleeping Beauty Castle** that houses **The Dragon's Lair** *(La Tanière du Dragon)* and **Sleeping Beauty's Gallery** *(La Galerie de la Belle au Bois Dormant)*. These are both great detailed walk-through attractions. The Dragon's Lair contains a huge animatronic dragon that may be frightening for children.

Top Tip: Fantasyland closes one hour before the rest of the park each day to clear the area for the nightly fireworks show.

Peter Pan's Flight

| FP Yes | None | 📷 No | ✓ 4 minutes | ⏳ 60 to 90 minutes |

Peter Pan's Flight is one of Disneyland Paris' most popular rides. It features beloved characters, it is a family-friendly and provides a small thrill too.

Hop aboard a flying pirate ship and take a voyage through the world of Peter Pan and Never Never Land.

As you soar, you will see scenes to the sides and underneath you, in a retelling of the classic story.

The ride's interior is stunning from the moment you step inside and truly immersive.

This is an incredibly popular ride, so we strongly recommend using Fastpass to avoid a long wait.

Alternatively, visit the attraction early in the morning, in the evening before Fantasyland closes, or during the parade. On busy days, Fastpasses will run out by midday.

Important: Visitors who are afraid of heights may find this ride unsuitable. The flying ships you sit in give the sensation of flight, and at times you will be several metres off the ground and descending steeply (albeit not too quickly). These sensations may surprise some guests – mostly, though, it seems to be adults who are affected by this, and not children.

Alice's Curious Labyrinth

🎫 FP	No	📏 None	📷 No	⌄ 10 minutes	⏳ None - Walkthrough

Ever fancied getting lost in the world of Alice in Wonderland? Well, now you can do precisely that!

This maze has a good variety of elements and is just challenging enough to keep you guessing where to go next. There are photo opportunities along the way too.

Once you reach the end of the maze, you have the option of returning to the park or climbing the Queen's Castle first. The climb is worth doing for the stunning view over the park. The labyrinth is great family fun and a good way for the little ones to burn some energy.

Lancelot's Carousel

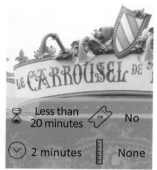

⏳ Less than 20 minutes	🎫 FP No
⌄ 2 minutes	📏 None

This is a beautiful, vintage carousel lined with golden horses, and is a joy to ride for every member of the family.

Whether you want to go along with the theme of Lancelot's carousel or prefer to think of it as the carousel from Mary Poppins, it is sure to be a fun-filled family adventure.

Meet Mickey Mouse

🎫 FP No	📏 None	📷 Yes	⌄ 1 to 2 minutes	⏳ 60 to 90 minutes

Mickey is preparing backstage for his next magic show, and you have the chance to meet him. While queuing in the indoor area, you could watch short films playing on a big screen.

Once you reach the front, you will enter a room with Mickey. Here you can meet the big cheese, have a chat, and get an autograph and photos.

You are welcome to take your own photos or ask the Cast Member present to help you. In addition, there is a Disney photographer there who will also take an official photo, which can be purchased at the attraction's exit.

"it's a small world"

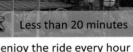

FUN FACT

This ride has more audio-animatronics that any other attraction at Disneyland Paris.

FP No	None	📷 No	✓ 10 minutes	⏳ Less than 20 minutes

"it's a small world" is one of the resort's most memorable and popular attractions, featuring hundreds of dolls singing a song about the uniting of the world.

We can guarantee you will get the melody stuck in your head.

Guests board a boat and travel leisurely through scenes depicting countries from around the world, as the attraction's song plays in various languages.

The loading system is incredibly efficient on this ride, meaning that the number of people who can

enjoy the ride every hour is high – this means that queues are often short.

This ride is a great Disney classic that is one of the "must-dos" for many visitors, even though it is not based on any film franchise.

Blanche Neige et les Sept Nains

Mad Hatter's Teacups

FP No	None	📷 No	✓ 2 minutes	⏳ 20 to 40 minutes

⏳ Less than 30 mins	FP No
✓ 2 minutes	None

Relive the tale of Snow White for yourself in this classic ride filled with light-hearted scenes, as well as many darker scenes too.

In the U.S.A., this same ride is called "Snow White's Scary Adventures", which gives you an idea of the scare level of the ride.

The Evil Witch, in particular,

makes surprise appearances out of every corner, the dark woods have ominous trees, and thunder and lightning effects may startle younger children.

Although the ride itself is slow-moving, the loud noises and the Evil Witch character are likely to scare young children.

Hop inside a teacup and go for a wild spin with the Mad Hatter.

The ride functions much like any other teacup ride around the world, where you have a wheel at the centre of the cup that you can turn to spin yourself round faster. Or, leave it alone and have a more relaxing spin.

Sleeping Beauty Castle - *Le Château de la Belle au Bois Dormant*

Standing 51m (167ft) tall, *Le Château de la Belle au Bois Dormant*, is the centrepiece and icon of Disneyland Park.

When the Imagineers were designing Disneyland Park, they knew that the castle here had to be different and unlike the castles in the American Disney theme parks. The European audience was accustomed to seeing real castles, and therefore, the park's icon had to be more fairytale-inspired than real.

The attention to detail is stunning, even including little snails (or *escargots*) on the turrets at the top, and the trees in front of the castle are cut into a square shape just like in the 1959 'Sleeping Beauty' film.

The castle is not just for show, however, and can actually be explored by guests. On the ground floor, you can walk along the drawbridge and over the moat to enjoy this magical building from the inside.

To the right-hand side of the castle, you can see a small wishing well where characters occasionally meet.

Behind the castle, you can find the **Sword in the Stone**. Try to remove it if you can, and be crowned king or queen of the kingdom.

Inside the castle, you can enjoy two unique shops, which are incredibly well-themed: enjoy Merlin the Magician's shop on the left, and a year-round Christmas shop on the right.

Once you have completed your shopping, take the winding staircase up the first floor and see the story of Sleeping Beauty retold using tapestries and beautiful **stained-glass windows**. You can even step foot onto the balcony outside for a stunning view over Fantasyland.

The castle's biggest secret, however, is altogether more hidden. When looking at the castle from the front, instead of taking the drawbridge, take the path on the left instead. This will lead you through a dark passageway and underground into **The Dragon's Lair**.

Here lies an enormous animatronic dragon (at the time, the biggest in the world) in an area unlike any other Disney theme park around the world. Every few minutes, the dragon comes to life. You can also access the lair through Merlin's shop.

Dumbo - The Flying Elephant

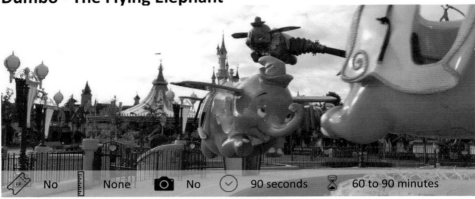

| FP | No | ▯ None | 📷 No | ⌄ 90 seconds | ⧖ 60 to 90 minutes |

Dumbo is one of the most popular rides in the whole of Disneyland Paris across the two parks.

Situated right in the centre of Fantasyland, it offers views of the surrounding area and is a lot of fun.

In front of the seats in each flying elephant, there is a lever that allows you to lift your Dumbo up or down and fly up to 7 metres (23ft) high!

As the ride is popular and has a low capacity, there are long waits all day from this attraction.

Ride it during the parade, during Extra Magic Time, or at the start or end of the day for the shortest waits. The ride handles just a third of the guests per hour that 'Pirates of the Caribbean' does.

The Adventures of Pinocchio

| FP | No | ▯ None | 📷 No | ⌄ 2 minutes | ⧖ 20 to 45 minutes |

Ride through a retelling of the story of Pinocchio and see the tales from the book and film come to life.

As with the original story, there are also some darker moments that may frighten younger children, though these do pass by quickly. It is much less frightening than Snow White's attraction, for example.

This ride is not a major attraction like *Peter Pan's Flight,* but it still draws in moderately sized queues due to the popularity of the characters.

Casey Jr: The Circus Train

No	None	No	2 minutes	20 to 45 minutes

Based on the character from Dumbo, Casey Junior is the little circus train that will take you on a ride around models of sets from classic Disney films.

This is a great ride for the whole family, and although it is not a roller coaster, it can be a good way of seeing whether the kids (or adults) are up to a slightly wilder ride, though this ride is still very tame compared to

the other coasters at the parks. Note that adults may feel a bit cramped on this ride with minimal leg and headroom.

There is no height restriction, so everyone can ride, and the low speed is unlikely to frighten anyone.

You will whiz by castles and other story pieces from Disney's classic tales during your ride. For a more

leisurely view of these scenes, try the Storybook Canal Boats located next door.

Unfortunately, the ride is often closed or only opened for limited periods during the off-season. It also usually closes two to three hours before the rest of Fantasyland.

Princess Pavilion

No	None	Yes	2 minutes	60 to 90 minutes

The Princess Pavilion is your chance to meet one of the Disney princesses. Then chat, play, get an autograph and take some photos.

Outside the attraction, there is a sign that will inform you of which princesses

you will meet at the end of the queue and the time each princess is available for meet and greets.

If seeing a particular princess is a priority, we suggest you visit the *Princess Pavilion* as early

as possible, as queue lines build up quickly.

Note that queues for this attraction can be long from the start of the day as it operates during Extra Magic Times.

Le Pays des Contes de Fees - **Storybook Canal Boats**

FP No	None	📷 No	✓ 2 minutes	⧗ Less than 20 minutes

This is a nice, relaxing ride, where you sail by models of classic childhood tales in a boat.

Along your serene journey, you will see scenes from the Little Mermaid, Hansel and Gretel, Fantasia, Snow White, the Wizard of Oz and many more films.

You will even enter the famous cave from Aladdin, and see the Genie's lamp shining brightly.

It is a nice change of pace from some of the busier attractions in the park, and you can take some great photos of the models.

This is a great attraction for very young children who can look around without anything potentially being scary.

If you want a different perspective on these same scenes, and a faster pace, consider riding Casey Junior instead.

This attraction almost always has low wait times, and many people do not seem to know this section of the park exists.

This attraction usually closes two to three hours before the rest of Fantasyland and may be closed during the off-season.

DINING

Auberge de Cendrillon – Table Service. This is a restaurant where all the Disney Princesses (and their accompanying princes) are present. They will perform dances throughout the meal, and visit every table to meet guests too. The adult set menu is priced at €77 and children's set menu is priced at €45. This meal can be pre-booked and pre-paid as part of a Disneyland Paris package and is also included on the Premium Meal Plan.

Au Chalet de la Marionette – Counter Service. Set menus are priced between €14 and €17, the children's set menu is priced at €9.

Pizzeria Bella Notte – Counter Service. Set menus are priced between €14 and €17, the children's set menu is €9. Serves pizza, rigatoni pasta and lasagne.

Toad Hall Restaurant – Counter Service. Set menus are priced at €14 to €17, the children's set menu is €9. Serves fish and chips, and chicken sandwiches.

The Old Mill – Snack location. Serves waffles (gaufres) with/without chocolate (€3.80 to €4), crisps at €2.30, cake at €4, ice creams at €3.50 to €4, and hot & cold drinks.

Fantasia Gelati – Snack location. Serves Italian-style scoop ice cream. €3 to €4 per ice cream, €3 for a hot drink.

Discoveryland

Take a look into the future... from the minds of the past. Discoveryland is inspired by retro-futuristic visions of space and beyond.

Attractions

Some of the park's most popular and thrilling attractions are located in this land. In addition to the attractions listed below, you can go on a trip around the park at the **Disneyland Railroad** Discoveryland Station.

Star Wars Hyperspace Mountain: Rebel Mission

Hyperspace Mountain is a thrilling roller coaster through space, and it is our favourite coaster at the resort.

It is the only Space Mountain in the world to have inversions and loops, as well as a high-speed launch. It is also the grandest and most extreme of all the Space Mountain rides around the world, and the beautiful steampunk-style building is the centrepiece for Discoveryland.

At the moment, this ride has a Star Wars overlay so you can expect to see ships from the hit series of films as you soar through space, as well as comets, supernovas,

Yes   1.20m   Yes   2 minutes

meteorites and other elements from the Star Wars saga, before landing back in Discoveryland. A must-do ride for thrill-seekers!

Top Tip: This ride has a

Single Rider queue line, so if you are alone, or do not mind being separated from your party, you can use it drastically reduce your wait time.

Average wait: 60-90 mins

Mickey's PhilharMagic - Discoveryland Theatre

Philharmagic is a fun 4D show for all the family.

The story is that you are attending Goofy's opera performance with Mickey's Philharmonic orchestra. When Donald gets involved,

however, things get a little out of hand, and you end up on an adventure travelling through a world of Disney classic movies.

With an air-conditioned queue line and theatre,

shelter from the rain and a fantastic musical movie, it is easy to see why this attraction is one of our favourites. However, waits are usually non-existent as shows run continuously throughout the day.

Les Mystères de Nautilus

| No | None | No | 5 minutes | ⧖ None - Walkthrough |

Explore Captain Nemo's ship, the Nautilus, from "20,000 Leagues under the Sea".

This incredibly detailed walkthrough takes you under the sea and into the heart of the captain's submarine.

This attraction truly is a fantastic work of art and includes some special effects inside such as a giant squid attack, as well as an incredible level of theming and detail.

Kids are unlikely to be entertained, however, as it is a simple walkthrough.

Be aware that some of the effects like the engine room may startle younger members of the family. It is also a bit dark in certain sections inside, but manageable for most people.

Insider Secret: Although you may believe you are inside the Nautilus ship, the winding staircase you use to enter this attraction is designed to disorientate you. Instead of walking towards the ship, you are actually walking down a long corridor and into a show building located between Autopia and Discoveryland Theatre – the exact opposite direction from the Nautilus.

Autopia

| No | See Below | No | 5 minutes | ⧖ 60 to 90 minutes |

Hop aboard one of these little cars and take it for a spin around Discoveryland.

Autopia is hugely popular with kids who get to drive a car for the very first time.

The cars are guided on rails so guests cannot go too far wrong, but the little ones (and bigger ones also) can steer and accelerate around the track and 'race' others.

The ride is great fun and is definitely worth a visit.

Riders under 0.81m may not ride. Riders between 0.81m and 1.32m must be accompanied by someone over the 1.32m height minimum. Riders over 1.32m may ride alone.

Star Tours: The Adventures Continue

 Yes 1.02m No ⌄ 5 minutes ⧗ 30 to 60 minutes

Star Wars fans will fall in love with *Star Tours*, but this attraction is equally fun for those who have never seen the films. This is a definite must-do.

Once in the queue line, you will enter an intergalactic spaceport, with adverts for various destinations and overhead announcements of flights leaving.

As you travel through the terminal, you will see Star-Speeders (your transport vehicle), an alien air traffic control station, R2-D2, C3PO, and many robots hard at work to make your journey to space unforgettable.

You will then board your StarSpeeder vehicle for your trip to one of many planets from the Star Wars universe.

With over 50 different randomised scenes, you never know what planet you will explore on your next ride.

Almost the entirety of the dialogue is in French, but it is the visuals along with the movement that really matter here; the simulator does feel incredibly realistic and this is a great ride.

Be advised that if you are

prone to motion sickness, or are scared of confined spaces, you should skip Star Tours.

Top Tip: If you want a milder ride, ask to be seated in the front row. This is the centre of the ride vehicle and therefore reduces the sensations felt. For a more thrilling experience, ask to be sat in the back row.

A permanent Star Wars character meet and greet location called "StarPort" is available in front of Star Tours featuring Darth Vador.

Orbitron: Machines Volantes

 No None No ⌄ 90 seconds ⧗ 30 to 60 minutes

Soar above Discoveryland in your very own spaceship.

This is a spinning-type ride similar to Dumbo in Fantasyland, but the ships here go higher, spin faster

and tilt more, making for a surprisingly good thrill.

It is a lot of fun, but it is not a must-do attraction and it is far from unique.

Note: It is a very tight fit for two adults in one spaceship, so avoid this. An adult and a child should fit in a spaceship fine, however.

Buzz Lightyear Laser Blast

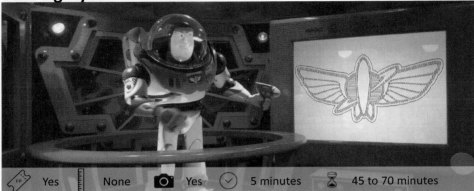

| | Yes | | None | | Yes | | 5 minutes | | 45 to 70 minutes |

On this interactive ride, once in your Space Cruiser, you can use its laser guns to shoot at the targets around you – you will be helping out Buzz Lightyear and racking up points.

Different targets are worth different amounts of points and there are even hidden targets so you can score thousands of bonus points.

At the end of the ride, the person with the most points wins. It is competitive, fun and endlessly re-rideable – it is also a great family adventure with no minimum height limit.

If you buy an attraction photo at the end, you can get your scores printed onto the photos too!

Top Tip: The highest scoring target is directly in front of Zurg – shoot his medallion repeatedly to get a huge number of points.

DINING

Cafe Hyperion – Counter Service. Adult set menus are priced at €14 to €17, and the children's set menu is €9.

Fireworks

Disney theme parks around the world are renowned for ending visitors' days by lighting up the sky with incredible firework displays. Disneyland Paris is no exception.

Disney Illuminations is Disneyland Paris' dazzling nighttime spectacular which coordinates music, projections, lasers, water fountains and fireworks.

Of all the nighttime spectaculars we have seen at Disney theme parks across the world, *Disney Illuminations* is one of the most impressive.

You can expect to see scenes from Star Wars, Frozen, Pirates of the Caribbean, The Little Mermaid, The Lion King and Finding Nemo.

Disney Illuminations is performed nightly at the closing of Disneyland Park. The show runs for 19 minutes. After the fireworks, Main Street, U.S.A. remains open for about 45 minutes after the park closes for your shopping convenience.

In addition, there are other fireworks shows offered on select nights such as Bastille Day and New Year's Eve. On these days, the themed firework display is first, followed by *Illuminations*.

Walt Disney Studios Park operates nighttime projection shows on the Hollywood Tower Hotel including during particular seasons such as Christmas and Season of the Force. There is also a fireworks display on New Year's Eve.

Lake Disney, by the on-site hotels, offers fireworks on select dates around Bonfire Night and on New Year's Eve too. Admission is free to Lake Disney.

DISNEY ILLUMINATIONS TOP TIPS:

1: For the best *Disney Illuminations* spot, we recommend you be in place at least 60 minutes before the show begins. Some guests get spots over an hour in advance.

2: Find a spot with a railing in front of you – this prevents someone from turning up during the show and obscuring your view. This often happens when guests put their children on their shoulders as the show begins, ruining the view for everyone behind. Equally frustrating is someone filming the show on their phone.

3: After the show, only Main Street, U.S.A. remains open. There are three main toilet locations for you to use – the first, and the least crowded, is located by the Baby Care Center (Zone J on the map overleaf). The second is inside the arcades running alongside Main Street. The third is at the end of Main Street, U.S.A. and to the right of the Disneyland Railroad station at the Arboretum (Zone P).

Disney Illuminations Viewing Guide

Disney Illuminations is primarily a projection show that relies heavily on you having a view of the front of Sleeping Beauty Castle.

Although the fireworks can be seen from across the park, you will not understand the show's storyline if you are not viewing the front of the

castle and its projections.

The front is also where the lasers, fountains and fire effects can be seen, as well as the Second Star to the Right effect on the castle.

You will want to position yourself at the central plaza (hub) area of the park or along Main Street, U.S.A. for

the best view.

To help you decide on the best view of *Disney Illuminations*, we have created this helpful guide – note that we have invented the zones or areas in the diagram and there are no delineations between the areas when you are in the park itself.

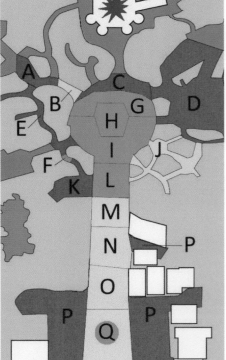

Zone A – A very off-centre view of the show. Uncrowded but a last resort.

Zone B – A better view than from Zone A. Uncrowded but an off-centre view. Good if you want to see the show last-minute from a decent angle. You may get wet here.

Zone C – Many guests sit or stand here, but this zone is too close to Sleeping Beauty Castle. You will miss some or all of the fireworks behind the castle. The projections do not have their full effect as you will be too close, and you will also likely get very wet from the water fountains.

Zone D – This area is often cleared by Cast Members and may or may not be open to guests. When the area is open, views are far from ideal and very off-centre.

Zone E – Views from this area are obstructed by trees, with no visibility.

Zone F – Located off-centre. Behind and to the left of the Disney Illuminations control booth. If you are positioned by the railing here, you will get a fantastic view of the show – this location can only accommodate a few people.

Zone G – This is where guests who arrive early will wait. This area provides a decent view of the show, and you will see all fireworks and effects. It is, however, still too close to the action for you to appreciate the show fully, in our opinion. Part of the area on the left of Zone G is reserved for people with disability cards and people accompanying them.

Zone H – Faces the castle head-on and is far back enough to provide a good view of the show. It is not a perfect view but it is very good.

Zone I – Our favourite view of the show. It is the perfect distance from Sleeping Beauty Castle. If you stand by the railings that surround the flowerbeds, you will have a near perfect view of the show. Be aware of the large speakers and light poles getting in the way.

Zone J – A very off-centre view with many trees meaning poor visibility. This is improved in the winter when there is less foliage and some spots can be decent. When the trees have leaves, this is not an acceptable viewing location.

Zone K – Views are obstructed by trees and the Disney Illuminations control booth. No visibility.

Zone L – An excellent view; it is a good distance from the castle to see the full show effects while not feeling too distant. This area is also usually less crowded than Zone I. You are also closer to the prk exit.

Zone M, N and O – These zones are located along Main Street, U.S.A. and provide an average view of the show. The closer you are to the Castle here, the better. These zones are usually less crowded than zones closer to the castle. You will likely see many people in front of you with kids on their shoulders.

Zone P – No visibility.

Zone Q – Must be staked out very early and involves you standing on the bandstand in Town Square – there is very limited space here but it provides an elevated view over other guests on Main street, U.S.A. Specific projections are hard to see from here but the unique view from this location makes it worth considering. It is not the way the show should be experienced the first time, however. At the end of the show, you are right by the park exit and well ahead of the crowds.

Disney Parades

Disney Stars on Parade is the best way to see all your favourite Disney characters in one place as they parade through Fantasyland, around the castle hub and down Main Street U.S.A.

The parade is performed daily and the time varies seasonally. Check the in-park Times Guide for the exact schedule.

Characters in the parade may vary from day to day but you can typically see about 50 different characters and floats, including: Tinker Bell, Toy Story characters, Simba, Nala, Baloo, Mowgli, Captain Hook, Peter Pan and characters from Finding Dory.

Other characters include Rapunzel, Cinderella, Snow White, Anna and Elsa.

It is not just the characters which are exciting though - one of the floats is a fire-breathing dragon which is sure to wow visitors.

The most popular place to watch the parade from is Main Street, U.S.A. You should secure your spot about one hour before the parade starts for the best view if watching from here.

The parade *is* not cancelled during light or moderate rain. During heavy rain, or if there is a thunderstorm alert, there is the potential for the parade to be cancelled or delayed. In either case, an announcement will be made at the parade start time.

Some other Disney theme parks feature a nighttime parade, in addition to a daytime one. Although

Disneyland Paris has done this in the past, this is not currently offered.

During seasonal events such as Spring, Halloween and Christmas, smaller parades with three to five-floats (dubbed cavalcades) are performed several times a day in addition to the main parade.

Walt Disney Studios Park

Walt Disney Studios Park is the second, and newest, theme park at Disneyland Paris. Here you can go behind the scenes and experience the magic of the movies.

Walt Disney Studios Park opened in 2002 and has significantly expanded over the years. In general, the park targets adolescents and adults more than young children and contains several thrill rides. There are also, of course, several attractions for the younger family members too.

Despite its expansion over the years, you would still be hard-pressed to spend an entire day in Walt Disney Studios Park due to the limited number of attractions. Disneyland Paris has stated that expanding the park and improving its offerings is a priority.

In 2014 *Ratatouille: The Adventure* was unveiled, a unique 3D trackless dark ride. Many more attractions and new areas of the park are set to arrive in the next few years.

At 5.3 million visitors per year, Walt Disney Studios Park is Europe's fourth most popular theme park, but still only receives half the number of visitors that its big brother, Disneyland Park, gets next door.

The park is divided into five main areas: Front Lot, Toon Studio, Production Courtyard, Toy Story Playland and Backlot.

Front Lot

As you enter the park, you are in Front Lot. This contains the Fantasia fountain as well as a covered area with shops and restaurants.

Front Lot is the entrance area to Walt Disney Studios Park, and home to *Disney Studio 1* – an indoor shopping and dining area designed to resemble Hollywood.

Disney Studio 1 is the equivalent of Main Street, U.S.A. in Disneyland Park. The façades of famous Hollywood buildings, as well as all the camera equipment, tell us that this isn't just a recreation, but a real working set designed to be used when making movies.

Sometimes there are pieces of street entertainment that are performed here. This area often offers face painting too (priced at €10 to €14).

Front Lot is home to Studio Services (Guest Services) where you can get assistance, make a complaint, leave positive feedback and apply for disability assistance cards. It is also home to Shutterbugs, the park's photography studio.

Once you have walked through Studio 1, you will see the Partners Statue with Mickey and Walt Disney holding hands - a great photo opportunity. Front Lot is also commonly home to photo spots with Disney characters.

Top Tip: If you are dining at Restaurant En Coulisse, look up - there is seating on the upper floor, which is open during busier times.

DINING:

Restaurant En Coulisse - Counter Service, adult set menus are €14 to €17, the children's set menu is €9. This restaurant runs on the right-hand side of Studio 1 behind several façades of famous movie sets.

The Hep Cat Corner - Snacks, serves hot and cold drinks for €3 to €4, a donut and drink combination deal is €6, ice creams are €3 to €4.

Production Courtyard

Attractions

Stitch Live!

 No None   No 15 minutes Until next show

Enter a special transmission room and before you know it, a Cast Member will connect you and your fellow earthlings in your theatre to Stitch and you will be speaking with him live in space.

Stitch is curious about how the planet Earth works, so he will ask all sorts of strange questions to learn about our home.

This attraction is good fun. There are separate English and French shows.

The Twilight Zone: Tower of Terror

 Yes 1.02m   Yes 2 minutes  60 to 90 minutes

The Twilight Zone: Tower of Terror transports you to the fifth dimension on the elevator ride of your life. You will see incredible special effects and feel what it is like to drop 124 feet (38m).

Disney summarises: "One stormy night long ago, five people stepped through the door of an elevator and into a nightmare. That door is opening once again, and this time it's opening for you."

You board a service elevator; learn the ghostly past of the hotel, and then *you* 'drop in'.

The elevator is like a free-fall ride, except that you are pulled down faster than gravity causing you to come out of your seat – don't worry, you have seatbelts!

Within a split second the elevator changes from going up to down, creating a weightless sensation unlike any other ride.

The atmosphere inside is truly immersive and is possibly the best theming

in all of Disneyland Paris. In addition, the Cast Members who work on this ride really add to the atmosphere.

This is a fun ride, but it is an intense experience that WILL have you screaming.

Studio Tram Tour: Behind the Magic

 No None No 15 minutes 30 to 60 minutes

Hop aboard a studio tram and see authentic props and vehicles from well-known movies, and sets close-up. During the ride you will experience fire, water and earthquakes, and see movie scenes in front of you.

Commentary is provided in English and French via screens on the tram.

This is a great family adventure for all ages.

DINING:

Restaurant des Stars – Buffet. The adult price is €35 with one drink; the children's buffet is €18 with one drink. Both buffets are included in the Standard Meal Plan.
Hollywood and Lime – Snack location. Drinks - €3 to €4, desserts - €3 to €4.

Backlot

Backlot is situated in the top-left hand corner of the park. In addition to the attractions below, you can also meet Spider-Man here.

Attractions

Rock 'n' Roller Coaster: Starring Aerosmith

 Yes   1.20m   Yes   90 seconds   20 to 45 minutes

Important: This ride will close permanently on 2nd September 2019 and will be replaced by a new Iron Man attraction (opening date tbc).

Hop aboard a SoundTracker and take a ride through an Aerosmith music video at over 55mph (90km/h) in this high-speed roller coaster.

The ride will take you through three inversions, 4.5Gs of Force and more - and it all starts with a catapult launch to the maximum speed in under 2.5 seconds. For each launch, there is a short light show, fog and a countdown.

There are several inversions, but the ride is incredibly smooth and comfortable.

Each vehicle plays a different set of Aerosmith songs from the song list.

This ride often has a surprisingly short wait time, even when the rest of the park is relatively busy.

Moteurs, Action! Stunt Show Spectacular

 No   None   No   40 minutes   Until next show

At *Moteurs, Action!* sit back and watch movie stunts be performed – and then learn how they are done!

This attraction is a major draw for many visitors and pulls in thousands of guests at a time, meaning that queues for other attractions are shorter when the show is being performed.

Arrive around 30 minutes before show-time to get a good seat. The middle seating section provides the best view, and the lower down you are, the closer you are to the action.

Although all seats do have a good view, being closer to the action makes the experience even more enjoyable.

DINING:

Cafe des Cascadeurs – Table/Quick Service Hybrid. Salads and sandwiches are €7 to €8, a set menu is €15, the children's menu is €9. Drinks, desserts and ice cream are also served.
Disney Blockbuster Cafe – Quick Service. A la carte sandwiches are priced at €8, pizzas are €9, salads and pasta are €7 to €8, drinks and desserts are €3 to €4. The set menu is €15.

Toon Studio

Discover the magic behind Disney cartoons and animation in this area of the park, from Disney classics to Pixar favourites.

Attractions

Crush's Coaster

No	1.07m	No	2 minutes	90 to 120 minutes

Journey through the East Australian Current with Crush in this fast and thrilling coaster.

Crush's Coaster is a unique attraction and the only of its kind in any Disney theme park worldwide.

Guests board turtle shells in groups of four, sat back-to-back in pairs. The ride starts relatively calmly as a dark ride with scenes, but it soon begins to build pace as the cars start their high-speed roller coaster sequence.

Most of the roller coaster portion is in darkness with effects scattered around the track to give you the feeling of riding the waves with Crush.

Although the ride may seem to target younger kids, do not be fooled - this is a wild, fast adventure, so read the warning signs outside first.

Some guests rate this as the most "thrilling" ride in the whole of Disneyland Paris, so it is a definite must-do for thrill -eekers!

The popularity of the characters and the ride's low hourly capacity means that this ride regularly has the second-longest queue in the entire park, after *Ratatouille*. The ride does not offer Fastpass.

Ride *Crush's Coaster* first thing in the morning or just before park closing for the shortest waits.

Even on less busy days, queues exceed 40 minutes and it is common to see the wait at over 90 minutes.

In the last hour before park closing, a long wait time is often displayed to discourage people from getting in the queue line.

Top Tip: A Single Rider queue is available; the wait time posted for this is often exaggerated so that guests choose to use the regular queue and the Single Rider line does not get too long.

Frozen Animation Celebration (Opening date: Winter 2019)

Previously home to Disney's Art of Animation, a new Frozen experience is set to open in late 2019.

This new attraction will be a mix of shows, meet and greets and other experiences.

Guests will move between three different rooms - the first is themed to a log cabin with Anna and Sven who are then joined by Elsa. Then you'll move to Elsa's Ice Palace for a sing-along. At the end, you will find Olaf who you can meet and get photos with.

Cars Quatre Roues Rallye

No	None	No	⌄ 90 seconds	⧖ 30 to 60 minutes

Hop in for a spin on Route 66 with the characters from Disney Pixar's *Cars*.

The ride is very similar to the teacups ride in Disneyland Park, but you spin faster in this version.

Vehicles can accommodate up to 2 adults, plus 2 extra kids.

Animagique Theater – "Mickey and the Magician"

No	None	No	30 minutes	⧖ Until next show

Go back in time to Paris at the turn of the 19th century... and enter a great Magician's workshop, where the assistant is none other than Mickey!

As well as the main cheese himself, you will see Tinker Bell from *Peter Pan*, Lumière from *Beauty and the Beast*, the Genie from *Aladdin*, the Fairy Godmother from *Cinderella*, Rafiki from *The Lion King*, and even Elsa from *Frozen*.

With unforgettable songs such as "Let it Go" and "Friend like Me", this is an unmissable spectacular. We think this is one of the best shows that Disneyland Paris has ever done - it is of West End theatre quality.

Flying Carpets over Agrabah

Yes	None	No	90 seconds	⧖ Less than 30 minutes

Board one of Aladdin's flying carpets and fly over Agrabah. As you soar through the skies, you will hear the Genie through his director's megaphone telling you how to act.

The ride itself is a simple spinner ride, and is very similar to both *Dumbo* and *Orbitron* (at Disneyland Park) – this ride, however, often has shorter queues.

Here you can raise and lower your carpet, and tilt it backwards and forwards!

Top Tip: It is very rare for the Fastpass machines to be activated on this ride.

Ratatouille: The Adventure

 Yes | None | No | ✓ 5 minutes | ⧗ 90 to 120 minutes

Ratatouille: The Adventure is the newest ride at Disneyland Paris. Here you board a 'ratmobile' and travel through the streets of Paris, scurrying along rooftops and kitchens in a clever 4D immersive ride.

Along your journey, your 3D glasses and giant screens put you in the heart of the action.

You can expect to feel the heat from a grill, the cold of a refrigerator, and you may even get splashed once or twice. There are also different smells throughout.

Ratatouille ride vehicles do not follow a track, taking slightly different paths for a unique experience each time.

As it is the newest attraction, this ride has the longest waits of both parks, and Fastpasses run out very quickly – usually within 30 minutes of park opening. In the last hour of park operation, an inflated wait time is often displayed to discourage people from queuing.

A Single Rider Line is available for this attraction.

This typically reduces wait times to less than 30 minutes and often to less than 15 minutes. On busy days, the wait for Single Rider may reach 60 minutes.

When disembarking your 'ratmobile' and returning your 3D glasses, look ahead for a glimpse into *Bistrot Chez Remy*, a restaurant where you are shrunk down to the size of a rat.

DINING:

Bistrot Chez Remy – Table Service. Set menus only. The Remy Menu is €33 for 2 courses (no dessert), Emile Menu is €41 for 3 courses, Linguini Menu is €49 for 2 courses (no dessert), Gustea Menu is €62 and is 3 courses with premium choices. The kids menu is €19 and a Premium Kids Menu is €35. The Gusteau menu and the Premium Kids Menu are on the Premium Meal Plan. The standard kids menu and the Emile Menu are on the Plus Meal Plan. Advanced reservations are recommended.

Toy Story Playland

Toy Story Playland shrinks you down to the size of a toy in Andy's back yard.

Attractions

Toy Soldiers Parachute Drop

FP No	0.81m	📷 No	✓ 1 minute	⏳ 60 to 90 minutes

Board one of the Toy Soldiers' parachutes and get ready to soar up into the sky and then glide back down to the ground again and again.

This is a great family ride and has become a new rite of passage for many.

Queues can get extremely long for this ride, so get here early.

Top Tip: A Single Rider queue line is available for guests happy to board individually.

Slinky Dog Zigzag Spin

FP No	None	📷 No	✓ 90 seconds	⏳ 20 to 45 minutes

Hop on Slinky Dog and enjoy yourself as you spin round and round in circles getting increasingly faster and faster.

This is a fun family-friendly attraction that is likely to entertain everyone from young toddlers to parents.

RC Racer

FP No	1.20m	No	1 minute	60 to 90 minutes

Hop on the RC car from Pixar's Toy Story films, and feel the wind in your hair as you ride both forwards and backwards along the car track.

The ride is great fun and a good adrenaline rush – it is often likened to the swinging pirate ships found at many theme parks, but we prefer the feeling on this.

Here, you are also secured by overhead harnesses, which you aren't on a pirate ship.

At the highest point, riders are 24m (80ft) high, and the free-fall feeling backwards is great fun.

The ride looks significantly more intimidating than it actually is and the sensation is not anywhere near as scary as it seems, in our opinion.

RC Racer has one of the most boring, and tedious, queues in all the park so we would recommend avoiding it if waits are long. It also moves very slowly.

Top Tip: A Single Rider queue is available for guests wishing to save time and board individually. Unfortunately, to get to this queue, you may have to wait in the normal queue line for a good while until the split point. This is because the Single Rider line only starts half-way into the regular queue.

Get here early to ride this attraction, as queues build up quickly, and the ride has a dismal hourly capacity - the lowest for any ride in the park.

PARADES AND FIREWORKS AT WALT DISNEY STUDIOS PARK:

Live entertainment at Walt Disney Studios Park is limited to the stage shows on offer such as *Mickey and the Magician* and *Moteurs, Action*.

Unfortunately, this park does not have a daytime or nighttime parade, nor does it have a nighttime show or fireworks. You will find the nightly fireworks show at Disneyland Park.

Exceptions: There is a firework show offered for guests at this park for the transition from New Year's Eve to New Year's Day at midnight. During *Season of the Force* and the Christmas Season, there is a nighttime spectacular projected onto *The Twilight Zone: Tower of Terror*'s building façades.

Touring Plans

Touring plans are easy-to-follow guides that minimise your waiting time in queue lines throughout the day. By following them, you can maximise your time in the parks and experience more attractions. There are several different touring plans available to suit your needs.

To see all of Disneyland Park, you will need to allocate at least two days. However, you *can* hit the headline attractions at the park in just one day if you are pressed for time. Walt Disney Studios Park can be seen in one day comfortably.

Unless you are going during an off-peak season, you will find it difficult to see the highlights from both parks in one day – there is not enough time.

These touring plans are not set in stone, so feel free to adapt them to the needs of your party. It is important to note that these plans focus on experiencing the rides; if your focus is on meeting all the characters

or seeing all the shows, then a touring plan is unlikely to be suitable for you. The only way to minimise waits for characters is to get to the parks and meet and greets early.

These touring plans are intense, BUT you will get to cram in as much as possible during your visit. If you are at the resort for multiple days, feel free to follow the plans at a more leisurely pace. Also, if you do not want to experience a particular ride, skip that step but do not change the order of the steps.

If an attraction is closed for refurbishment during your trip, skip those steps.

You must purchase your

tickets in advance to make the most of your time and these touring plans. If you need to buy a ticket on the day, turn up at least 30 minutes earlier than the recommended start times on these plans - and even earlier during peak season.

Insider Tip: To minimise the time you spend waiting in queue lines, you will often need to cross the park from one side to the other – this is purposely done by theme parks to disperse crowds more evenly. Note, for example, how the three roller coasters at Disneyland Park are all in different lands and far away from each other – the same also applies at Walt Disney Studios Park.

Disneyland Park

1 DAY PLAN FOR GUESTS WITH EXTRA MAGIC TIME:

Step 1: At 8:15am be at the park gates for entry - the park opens at 8:30am. Pick up a Park Map and a Times Guide under the archways of Main Street, U.S.A. Station. These list parade, show, character and firework times, as well as attraction closures. If you want to meet any characters do so now, before the rides. Walk down Main Street, U.S.A., get photos and proceed straight to *Sleeping Beauty Castle*.

Step 2: Enter Fantasyland and ride *Dumbo: The Flying Elephant* first, followed by *Peter Pan's Flight*. If you have an interest in meeting the Disney Princesses, then visit *Princess Pavilion.* If not, skip to step 3.

Step 3: If it is not yet 9:50am, ride *Lancelot's Carousel* and *Mad Hatter's Teacups*. You can ride these later if you are short on time, as queues are usually very short for both.

Step 4: By 9:50am, make your way back to the park's hub in front of the castle. Here, wait at the entrance to Frontierland with other guests.

Step 5: At 10:00am, when the park opens, go directly to B*ig Thunder Mountain*. Ride it.

Step 6: Visit Discoveryland and pick up a Fastpass for *Buzz Lightyear Laser Blast*.

Step 7: Now it is decision time – What do you fancy doing? a) Driving a car or b) A Rollercoaster through space. If you want to drive a car, walk over to *Autopia* in Discoveryland. Otherwise, visit *HyperSpace Mountain* in Discoveryland. Be prepared for a wait at both of these.

Step 8: If it is time, use your *Buzz Lightyear Laser Blast* Fastpass. If not, next decision: Do you fancy meeting Mickey Mouse, or going on a simulator ride into outer space? *Meet Mickey Mouse* in Fantasyland is the permanent home for the big cheese himself. Space adventurers should ride *Star Tours* in Discoveryland.

Step 9: If it is time, use your *Buzz Lightyear Laser Blast* Fastpass.

Step 10: Now is your chance to do any rides you have opted not to do so far. If, for example, you opted to go to *Autopia*

and *Star Tours*, then now is the time to go to *Meet Mickey Mouse* and *Princess Pavilion* (or vice-versa). Queues for these attractions will only continue to increase as the day progresses. Also, meet and greet locations shut several hours before the park closes.

Step 11: Grab some lunch.

Step 12: You now have a few rides left to do in Fantasyland. Experience *Casey Junior, Le Pays des Contes de Fees, Blanche Neige (Snow White)* and *Pinocchio*. Ride these one after another, in this order, if you want to do them all. *Casey Junior* and *Storybook* close several hours before the rest of the park.

Step 11: If any live shows such as *Frozen Sing-Along* or *Forest of Enchantment* are playing during your visit, you may want to watch these now.

Step 12: Is it time for the Parade yet? The parade is traditionally at 5:30pm but make sure to check your Times Guide for exact timings. Show up 45 minutes before or even earlier for a good spot on Main Street, U.S.A.

Step 12: Many people leave after the parade, so the park will be less busy. Now is the time to either take a bit of a rest on a bench to avoid burning out or to go on rides that have fast moving queues. Ride *Pirates of the Caribbean*.

Step 13: Ride *"it's a small world"*. This attraction handles thousands of guests an hour, so queues are always moving.

Step 14: Ride *Indiana Jones et le Temple du Peril*.

Step 15: Head to *Phantom Manor*. Explore the cemetery located by the ride exit for some great puns.

Step 16: Check when the night-time show *Disney Illuminations* is being presented. This should not to be missed!

Now depending on what time of the day it is, and when the park closes, it is either time to watch *Disney Illuminations*, have dinner or do the walkthrough attractions.

Walkthrough attractions do not have a waiting time. These include: *Adventure Isle and La Cabane des Robinson, Le Passage Enchante d'Aladdin, Alice's Curious Labyrinth* (closes early for the fireworks), and the wonderfully themed *Les Mystères de Nautilus*.

Step 17: Get a spot in front of the castle or on Main Street, U.S.A. at least 45 minutes before *Disney Illuminations* begins. See our section on *Disney Illuminations* at the end of the Disneyland Park chapter for help finding the perfect spot. We grab a hot dog from Casey's Corner whilst waiting to help the time pass.

Disneyland Park Touring Plan Notes

Two attractions that are not covered in these plans:
• *Thunder Mesa Riverboat Landing* - The wait time for this attraction is never longer than 30 minutes so you may be able to fit it in.
• *Disneyland Railroad* goes around the park. There are four different stations to board at, but the one with the shortest queues is usually Frontierland station as it is hidden away.

Be aware that both these

attractions stop operation well before the park closes.

Disneyland Paris also lists the following as attractions so you might want to fit them in at some point:

• *Horse-Drawn Streetcars*
• *Main Street Vehicles*
• The *Liberty* and *Discovery Arcades*

We do not feel these are must-dos, unless you have time to spare.

This guide does not take into account live shows, as those vary throughout the year, check your Times Guide for more. Be sure to watch them.

Also be sure to visit the *Gallery* inside Sleeping Beauty Castle (upstairs) and the *Dragon's Lair* underneath. Entry to Sleeping Beauty Castle ceases at least one hour before Disney Illuminations, as does all of Fantasyland.

1 DAY WITHOUT EXTRA MAGIC TIME - FOCUS: KIDS RIDES

Step 1: Arrive at 9:20am at Disneyland Park's entrance. Enter the park when it pre-opens at 9:30am. Until 10:00am you can shop, eat and ride the *Main Street Vehicles*. Pick up a Times Guide under the archways of *Main Street U.S.A. Station*. This contains parade, show, character and firework times, as well as attraction closures and park hours.

Step 2: Walk down Main Street, U.S.A., get photos and proceed straight to *Sleeping Beauty Castle*.

At Sleeping Beauty Castle's hub lies the entrance to all the lands of the park – Disney Hotel guests and some Annual Passholders will have access to the rest of the park at this time.

Stand by the rope leading to the castle. This rope is removed at 10:00am so all guests can go through.

Step 3: Get a *Peter Pan's Flight* Fastpass.

Step 4: Go to *Princess Pavilion* to meet a princess.

Step 5: Go to *Meet Mickey Mouse*.

Step 6: Use your *Peter Pan's Flight* Fastpass if it is time.

Step 7: Get a *Buzz Lightyear Laser Blast* Fastpass from Discoveryland.

Step 8: Have lunch.

Step 9: Ride *Dumbo: The Flying Elephant*. It will have long waits later.

Step 10: *Ride Casey Junior*.

Step 11: Ride *Le Pays des Contes de Fees* next.

Step 12: Ride *Pinocchio,* and *Snow White's Scary Adventures* in Fantasyland.

Step 13: Use your *Buzz Lightyear Laser Blast* Fastpass.

Step 14: Get a spot at least 45 minutes before the start of *Disney Stars on Parade* anywhere along the parade route. It is usually on at 5:30pm but be sure to check your Times Guide.

Step 15: Ride *Autopia* or explore inside *Sleeping Beauty Castle*. If there is a lot of time until park closing, do both. Fantasyland closes one hour before the other lands.

Step 16: Ride *"it's a small world"* in Fantasyland.

Step 17: Decision: *Explore Alice's Curious Labyrinth* or ride *Le Carousel de Lancelot*. If there is still a lot of time left until the park closes, do both.

Step 18: If any shows are playing, now is a great time to watch one.

Step 19: Ride *Pirates of the Caribbean* in Adventureland.

Step 20: Ride *Phantom Manor* in Frontierland.

Step 21: Have dinner and watch *Disney Illuminations*. Get a spot in front of the castle or on Main Street, U.S.A. at least 45 minutes before the show begins. See our section on *Disney Illuminations* to find the perfect spot.

Note: If your children want a thrill, *Big Thunder Mountain* in Frontierland should be your choice, as it does not go upside down and is the tamest roller coaster in the park.

1 DAY WITHOUT EXTRA MAGIC TIME - FOCUS: THRILLS

Step 1: Arrive at 9:20am at the entrance to Disneyland Park. Enter as the park pre-opens at 9:30am. Until 10:00am you can shop and eat on Main Street, U.S.A. and ride the *Main Street Vehicles*. Pick up a Times Guide under the archways of Main Street, U.S.A. Station. This contains parade, show, character meeting and firework times, as well as attraction closures and park hours.

Step 2: Walk down Main Street, U.S.A., get photos and proceed straight to *Sleeping Beauty Castle*.

At Sleeping Beauty Castle's hub lies the entrance to all the lands of the park – Disney Hotel guests and some Annual Passholders will have access to the rest of the park at this time.

Stand by the rope leading to Frontierland. This rope is removed at 10:00am so all guests can go through.

Step 3: Ride *Big Thunder Mountain* in Frontierland immediately as the park opens.

Step 4: Ride *Star Wars Hyperspace Mountain* in Discoveryland.

Step 5: Ride *Star Tours*.

Step 6: Ride *Indiana Jones et le Temple du Peril* in Adventureland. Now you have ridden all the roller coasters in this park.

Step 7: Ride *Pirates of the Caribbean*.

Step 8: Get a *Buzz Lightyear Laser Blast* FastPass in Discoveryland.

Step 9: Time for lunch.

Step 10: Ride *Autopia*.

Step 11: If it is time for your *Buzz Lightyear Laser Blast* Fastpass, use it or skip to step 12.

Step 12: Ride *"it's a small world"*.

Step 13: Get a *Peter Pan's Flight* Fastpass.

Step 14: Use your *Buzz Lightyear Laser Blast* Fastpass if it still has not been used.

Step 15: Get a spot at least 45 minutes before the beginning of *Disney Stars on Parade* on Main Street, U.S.A. or anywhere else along the parade route.

Step 16: If you are interested in watching any shows, now is a perfect time.

Step 17: Ride *Phantom Manor*.

Step 18: Explore *Les Mystères de Nautilus* and other walkthroughs such as *Le Passage Enchanté d'Aladdin* or *La Cabane des Robinson*.

Step 19: Use your *Peter Pan's Flight* Fastpass and explore *Alice's Curious Labyrinth*.

Step 20: Have dinner.

Step 21: Get a spot in front of the Castle or on Main Street, U.S.A. at least 45 minutes before *Disney Illuminations*. See our section on *Disney Illuminations* for help finding the perfect spot.

---

2 Day Disneyland Park Touring Plan:
If you want to experience everything Disneyland Park has on offer in two days, follow the 1-Day plan for 'Kids Rides' on one day, followed by the 1-Day plan for 'Thrill Rides' the next day. This will cover all the rides in the most logical sequence. Combine the touring plans with Extra Magic Time if you have that available to you and you should comfortably be able to experience Disneyland Park and all its attractions.

If you have three days or longer at Disneyland Park, there is no need to follow our touring plans rigidly. Make sure to arrive early, use Fastpass, and visit the busiest rides at the start or end of the day.

Walt Disney Studios Park

Important: Guests with Extra Magic Time access should ride *Crush's Coaster* first, followed by *Ratatouille*, then pick up this plan from Step 4.

Step 1: Arrive at the Walt Disney Studios Park entrance by 9:20am. Enter the park at 9:30am when it pre-opens. Get a Park Map and a Times Guide as you enter *Studio 1*. Walk through *Studio 1* briskly and do not waste time looking around - you can do that later.

Step 2: Pick up a Fastpass for *Ratatouille: The Adventure* as Fastpasses for this ride are distributed very quickly.

Step 3: Head to *Crush's Coaster*. Ride it. The wait may be long, but it will likely not get any shorter throughout the day.

Step 4: Visit Toy Story Playland. There are several attractions to experience here. Ride them in this order: *Toy Soldiers Parachute Drop, RC Racer* and *Slinky Dog*. Keep an eye on your *Ratatouille* Fastpass time.

Step 5: Ride *Cars Quatre Roues Rallye* – this is located opposite *Crush's Coaster*.

Step 6: Hopefully at least two hours will have elapsed since you picked up your Fastpass for *Ratatouille: The Adventure*, so go and pick up a Fastpass for *The Twilight Zone: Tower of Terror*.

Step 7: Fit lunch in around your Fastpass time for *Ratatouille: The Adventure*. If it is time to ride the attraction now, do that first. If not, have lunch and return to use your Fastpass.

Step 8: Ride *Rock n' Roller Coaster (closes Sep 2019)*. If *Animation Celebration* is open (starting late 2019), experience this.

Step 9: Ride *Studio Tram Tour*.

Step 10: Ride *Flying Carpets over Agrabah*.

Step 11: Use your *Tower of Terror* Fastpass if it is time. If it is not, then skip forward to step 13 and fit *Tower of Terror* in around the showtimes.

Step 12: That is it for all the rides. This park is tiny in comparison to Disneyland Park.

As well as the character meets, there are three main shows left to experience, so take these in according to their schedules which are available in the Times Guide which you picked up at the start of the day.

These shows are:
• *Lights, Motors, Action*
• *Stitch Live*
• *Mickey & The Magician*

Outside the Parks

A trip to Disneyland Paris isn't just about the theme parks - there are a wealth of things to do outside the parks such as the shopping district, Disney Village. Plus, the fun does not have to stop at the resort. After all, you are near one of Europe's largest and most vibrant cities. Also, there are opportunities for shopping and other adventures nearby.

Disney Village

Disney Village is an entertainment district located just next to the theme parks and on-site hotels where you can continue the fun into the night after the parks close. This area houses a live show, a cinema, restaurants, shops, bars and more. Admission to Disney Village is free.

ENTERTAINMENT:

Buffalo Bill's Wild West Show

Located at the entrance to Disney Village, *Buffalo Bill's* is a dinner show starring Mickey and the gang as they venture through the Wild West. The show lasts 90 minutes, and features live animals, Disney characters, stunts and some great sets! The show is a great way to spend an evening, combining live entertainment and a meal.

Pricing:
Category one seating is €80, and category two seating is €65 per adult. Children's prices are €17 less per person. You should compare the cost to a visit to a theatre show – here you get a show and a meal for one price.

Category 2 is further away from the action than Category 1. Category 1 seating also includes a non-alcoholic welcome cocktail, and treats with your tea or coffee at dessert time.

The food:
The adult meal consists of a roast chicken drumstick, sausage, potato wedges, ice cream and unlimited drink refills (beer or non-alcoholic beverages), as well as dessert and tea and coffee. There is a separate kids menu. All the food and drinks are included in the price, and this is served family-style. Food offerings are subject to change.

There are two showings per night – at 18:30 and 21:30 – and the show only operates on select days each week.

More information:
If you are allergic to dust or animals, do not attend this show.

Access to under 18s is not permitted unless they are accompanied by an adult. Alcohol will only be served for guests aged 18 or over – ID may be required.

Panoramagique

Soar into the sky and get a bird's-eye view of Disneyland Paris from the world's largest helium-filled passenger balloon – *Panoramagique*.

This is a great way to take some photos of the resort where you can clearly see everything around you, including both theme parks, Disney Village and the resort hotels.

It truly is a unique perspective from where you can appreciate all the different activities on offer at the resort.

Pricing is €12 per adult and €6 per child for the flight. A meal deal which includes a flight on *Panoramagique* and a meal at *Earl of Sandwich* is also available.

Note that flights do not operate in periods of high wind, or adverse weather conditions.

La Marina

La Marina offers water activities from rowing boats to pedal boats, and electric boats to hydro bikes. Land-based activities are also available such as surrey bikes which you can hire. Activities operate at a charge and are based on weather conditions.

Operating times are 16:00 to 22:00 daily during high season (school holidays) and on weekends. Activities may also be available at other times.

Pricing:
* *Electric boat hire* – €20 for 20 minutes, 5 people maximum per boat
* *Hydro Bikes* – €5 for 20 minutes, 1 person per bike. Minimum age: 12.
* *Pedal Boats* – €10 for 20 minutes, 5 people maximum per boat.
* *Surrey bike* – €10 for 20 minutes for a 2-adult + 1 child bike, or €15 for 20 minutes for a 4-adult + 1 child bike.

MORE ENTERTAINMENT:
• **Disney Stadium** - In between the Disney Store and the Sports Bar, the Disney Stadium is where you can choose from a series of classic arcade-style video games, as well as air-hockey. Games are mostly priced at €2 each.
• **Sports Bar** - Being at Disneyland Paris does not mean missing out on your favourite sporting events. Go to the Sports Bar and watch the game on the huge screen, while having a drink or two and a snack. The Sports Bar also hosts weekly karaoke sessions and other forms of live entertainment open to all at no cost.
• **Billy Bob's** - As well as a restaurant during the day, Billy Bob's is a bar and nightclub when the night draws in. Children are allowed in at all times of the day and night, except during some adult-only events. Cast Members often frequent the bar at the end of a hard day's work in the parks – here drinks are free-flowing and adults and children alike can dance the night away.
• **Cinema Gaumont** - With 15 different auditoriums, including one with an IMAX screen, there is bound to be something for you to enjoy watching at this cinema. You can check film schedules in advance at http://bit.ly/dlpcinema. Films listed as VOST (usually only one) are shown in their original language (often English) with French subtitles.

DINING:

Disney Village has a variety of dining options, from Quick Service (fast food), to Character Dining options (Disney characters visit each table while you eat) to more traditional Table Service restaurants (order from a menu and your food is brought by a waiter).

McDonald's – Quick Service. McDonald's is a well-known fast-food chain, but this branch has inflated prices due to the location. A standard meal costs between €8 and €9, with a child's meal costing about €5. Be aware that queues can be long if you do not use the automated terminals and want to order from an employee instead. The terminals can be set to English easily and accept bank cards but not cash, and we highly recommend using these.

Starbucks Coffee – Quick Service. This is a standard Starbucks location. However, it should be noted that Starbucks is not cheap in France, and this location is no exception. A hot or cold brewed drink is priced between €4 and €6, and sandwiches are about €5.

Earl of Sandwich – Quick Service. Prices are about €7 for a "gourmet" heated sandwich and €8 for a salad. The adult sandwich set menu is €11.50, with a kids' set menu at €7.50.

An "Adult Balloon Flight" meal is available for €18.50 and includes a warm sandwich, crisps, a soft drink or bottle of water,

a chocolate brownie or cookie, and one flight on *Panoramagique*. A "Child Balloon Flight" meal is €10.50 and includes a mini-sandwich, a soft drink or bottle of water, a mini chocolate brownie or fruit cup, and one flight aboard Panoramagique.

Cafe Mickey – Table Service. The adult set menu is €65, and the kid's set menu is €35; both are on the Premium meal plan. Characters are present at dinner time.

Annette's Diner – Table Service. The American-style breakfast menu is €14. There are several all-day set menus at €20, €30 and €37. The children's set menu is €18. Main courses are €17 to €27 a la carte. Milkshakes are €10 to €11. The children's set menu and €37 adult set menu are both on the Plus Meal Plan.

King Ludwig's Castle – Table Service. Here there is a special lunch menu (dish of the day style) served until 5:00pm priced at €15. There are also standard set menus at €24 and €27 with

no drinks. Main courses are €16.50 to €27 a la carte.

Planet Hollywood – Table Service. Main courses are €15 to €33. The kids' set menu is €12.50.

Rainforest Cafe – Table Service with a unique rainforest-like ambience. Main courses are €19 to €33. The 2-course set menu is €24.

The Steakhouse – Table Service. Adult set menus are €33, €39, €44 and €56. A la carte menu items are €27 to €60. The children's menu is €19, with a premium kids' set menu at €36. The €19 children's set menu and the €39 adult set menu are both in the Plus Meal Plan. Guests with the Premium Meal Plan can order anything from the menu a la carte (or the kids' premium set menu).

New York Style Sandwiches – Quick Service and snack location. The set menus are €10 to €15. The children's menu is €9. This location also serves hot and cold drinks, and ice creams.

Billy Bob's Country Western Saloon – Billy Bob's is divided into two dining establishments – *Bar Snacks*, a snack and Quick Service location, and *La Grange*, an all-you-can-eat Tex Mex buffet. The bar snacks set menu is €14 for adults and €8 for children. A la carte items are €2.50 to €9.50. The La Grange buffet is €35 with one drink, and €18 per child with one drink.

Sports Bar – Quick Service and Snacks. Snacks are served until 11:00pm. Sandwiches and burgers are €9 to €11. Other selected warm dishes include pasta bolognese, hot dogs and fish and chips priced between €8 and €11. Pizzas are €12 to €14. An adult sports bar menu is €14, along with a children's menu at €8.

Vapiano – Quick service. Amazingly fresh food. Pick a seat, then order your pizza or pasta from a food station, it's made fresh in front of you in minutes — our favourite fast food location in Disney Village. Main courses are €11 to €14.

Five Guys Burgers – Quick service. The best burgers at Disneyland Paris, in our opinion. Expect to pay €6 to €10 for a burger. Fries and drinks are extra.

SHOPPING:

After a meal, you may want to treat yourself with a little bit of retail therapy; here you are spoilt for choice with several merchandise locations.

World of Disney – As you walk into Disney Village from the parks, this is the first store you see. *World Of Disney* is the best place to get your Disney merchandise outside of the theme parks. It is also the largest store at the resort, featuring a beautiful interior, plenty of tills to pay at, and a good selection of merchandise.

The Disney Store – This classic location is a traditional-style Disney store. Uniquely, here you can create your own lightsabers, and your own Mr Potatohead figure, as well as purchase from a selection of more common Disney merchandise.

Planet Hollywood Store – Get items with the Planet Hollywood brand on them. This store mainly stocks apparel.

The Disney Gallery – This location features collector's items such as figurines and paintings. Also, you can take advantage of Disney's *Art on Demand* kiosks, where you can order a poster from an interactive display. This poster is then created and delivered to your home. With over 200 different posters to choose from, there is something for everyone.

LEGO Store – This is the largest LEGO store in France. It features all kinds of different LEGO sets, but unfortunately, it does not feature any exclusive Disney-themed merchandise. Nevertheless, it is worth a visit for fans of the colourful bricks.

Disney Fashion – For fans of Disney clothing, this is your haven.

World of Toys – This store is *the* place to buy princess dresses, dolls, and sweets.

Rainforest Café Store – The perfect place to get all your Rainforest Café branded merchandise.

Paris

Disneyland Paris is located a mere 35 minutes away from the centre of Paris by train, so visiting the 'City of Lights' should be considered on an extended trip.

Paris is filled with monuments, museums, rich culture and history. You should try to visit some of the following world-class attractions during your time in the city: the Eiffel Tower, the *Louvre* museum, *Musée d'Orsay, Arc de Triomphe, Champs Elysées, Montmartre* and the *Sacre Coeur* church.

Museums are reasonably priced, and European Economic Area citizens aged under 26 get free entry to most museums in the city. In addition, non-EEA visitors under the age of 18 get free entry with ID. There are even monthly openings of the museums with free admission for everyone, regardless of age.

We recommend taking a river cruise on the river Seine or a bus tour, which will allow you to see several monuments in one go.

If you wish to visit several attractions and get unlimited public transport, the Paris Pass is worth considering.

To get to central Paris, catch the RER A train from *Marne-la-Vallee – Chessy* station, located just a two-minute walk from the parks. Once you are in the centre of Paris, you may need to use the metro to get to various destinations.

A Mobilis day pass is the best travel ticket (priced at €17.80 for zones 1 to 5). It allows unlimited travel until midnight on Paris' transport system within Paris, and to and from Disneyland Paris.

Disneyland Paris sells several excursions to Paris:

Paris Essentials – A free-style tour with time to explore alone. It includes a return coach trip from Disneyland Paris and a river cruise in Paris. Prices are €49 per adult and €39 per child. The tour runs between 10:30am and 7:15pm (8:45pm in summer).

Paris Eiffel Tower to Notre Dame – Includes a return coach trip from Disneyland Paris, access to the Eiffel Tower, a river cruise and 90 mins free time near Notre Dame. The tour costs €120 per adult and €99 per child. It runs at the same times as the previous tour.

Magical Day Tour of Paris – Return coach transport from Disneyland Paris, highlights city tour on coach. Then you will visit the second floor of the Eiffel

Tower with a cruise or have time to explore the Louvre. Prices are €95-€110 per adult and €75-€99 per child, depending on the options selected. This tour departs at 9:45am and returns at 7:15pm.

Versailles & Paris Tour – Return coach transport from Disneyland Paris, entry to Versailles palace, transfer to city centre, and river cruise. Prices are €109 per adult and €79 per child. This tour departs at 10:30am and returns at 8:30pm.

Paris Illuminations and Eiffel Tower Tour – Return coach trip from Disneyland Paris to central Paris with a 90-minute on-coach tour, plis entry to the Eiffel tower. Prices are €90 per adult and €75 per child. The tour runs from 7:30pm to midnight.

Ratatouille Day Trip – Return transport, coach city highlights tour, lunch cruise and virtual flying experience. Priced at €149 per adult and €129 per child. Runs from 9:45am to 7:15pm

Val d'Europe

Located minutes away from Disneyland Paris is *Val d'Europe* - a new town designed by Disney with a huge shopping centre.

It is only one stop away on the RER A line train (€1.95 per journey). Trains run every 10 minutes with a journey time of about 2 minutes.

Alternatively, you can catch the number 50 bus which is free from just outside *Marne la Vallée - Chessy* train station.

If you are taking the bus, you will exit at the last stop by the *Hotel l'Elysée*. Cross the road at the pedestrian crossing and the shopping centre is in front of you. These buses run somewhat infrequently during the day.

If using the RER train, make sure to leave *Val d'Europe* station through the exits marked *Centre Commercial*.

Outside the station, turn right and walk straight ahead, crossing the road. The shopping centre will be in front of you. Note that it is closed on some public holidays. Shops are open from 10:00am until 9:00pm from Monday to Saturday (and close at 8:00pm on Sunday), with restaurants staying open until midnight daily.

If you would like to stock up on groceries, there is a huge supermarket in the shopping centre, as well as SeaLife aquarium (entry is €16 to €21 per person), and many other stores.

Follow the signs to *La Vallée Village* outlets for designer luxury goods at reduced prices.

Villages Nature

Villages Nature is a partnership between Disneyland Paris and *Pierre et Vacances*. It is located 15 minutes from the main Disneyland Paris site.

This new eco-tourism location has been built around a geothermal lagoon. It features apartment-style accommodation, numerous restaurants to enjoy and recreation options.

A shuttle bus runs between *Villages Nature* and Disneyland Paris, and you can book accommodation packages to stay at Villages Nature and play at Disneyland Paris.

The Aqualagoon (an indoor water park) features giant water slides, a wave pool, and an outdoor lagoon heated to 30°C year round. This is open daily from 10:00am to 8:45pm.

Also on offer: BelleVie Farm hosts educational programs and workshops; Extraordinary Gardens is a set of four landscaped gardens inspired by the Four Elements; Forest of Legends is a huge outdoor playground; Treeclimbing trails; a bowling alley; boutiques; cultural events and much more.

If you are not staying at the accommodation, you can buy a day pass to visit this unique location for €50 per adult and €40 per child. On certain days you can also buy a half-day pass which allows access from 5:00pm to 11:00pm. Parking is an extra €10. Accommodation starts at €225 for 2 nights.

Davy Crockett's Adventure

If you like adventure assault courses, you will love Davy Crockett's Adventure! There are swings, trapezes, rope bridges, ladders and much more for you to explore, making this High Rope location great family fun.

This attraction is located at the entrance to Davy Crockett Ranch – a campsite run by Disneyland Paris and considered one of the seven on-site hotels. It is 8km from the central resort hub.

This activity is open seasonally – you should visit www.aventure-aventure.com (French only) for opening times (Under 'Pratique' and then 'Horaires'). The assault courses are operated by a third-party company and not Disneyland Paris.

Note there is no shuttle bus to the Davy Crockett Campsite where this activity is located. You will need a car if you wish to participate in the experience, or alternatively you can book a taxi.

Golf Disneyland

Golf Disneyland is a world-class 27-hole golf course located right on Disneyland Paris property and open to all visitors, including hotel and day guests. You can rent out golf equipment and have a go yourself or watch others play.

Green fees for 18 holes start at €50 per person on weekdays and €75 on weekends. 9 holes costs €35 and €45 respectively. A reduced rate for the 18-hole course is available for those aged under 25. The golf course is open year-round, except on Christmas Day and New Year's Day. Club rentals are €27 for a complete set, or €5 per club.

A restaurant and bar overlook the course, and golf cart hire is available too.

The Pro Shop is also on-site, which sells a large variety of golfing gear. Lessons are also available.

To make a reservation you can email dlp.golf.disneyland@disney.com or call +33 (0) 1 60 45 68 90.

Guests with Disabilities

Disneyland Paris is a place designed to be enjoyed by everyone, regardless of their mental or physical abilities and over 60,000 disabled guests visit yearly.

Accessibility Cards

Parties of guests with disabilities should stop by Guest Relations at either park on the first day of their visit. In Disneyland Park, this is City Hall (on the left after the train station), and at Walt Disney Studios Park this is at Studio Services (on the right before Studio 1).

At Guest Relations, guests who have a disability (permanent or temporary), and expectant mothers, can apply for one of two cards that will facilitate their visit: the Priority Card and the Easy Access Card.

The **Priority Card** allows a permanently disabled guest and up to 4 members of their party access to attractions via a specially adapted entrance. This entrance will involve less walking and no stairs. It could be through the ride's exit, through the Fastpass entrance or a specially adapted queue line. In cases that the standard queue line is adapted, you will use the standard access. Entry procedures vary from ride to ride – to learn the boarding options available to you at each attraction, ask a Cast Member at the ride entrance.

This card does not provide instant access; wait times vary based on the number of people in the Priority Card queue. To receive the card, the disabled person (or their helper) must present supporting documents or a medical certificate. Proof of ID is required and may be requested when boarding rides.

Supporting documentation to prove disability for guests from France includes one of the following: disability card, disabled person's priority card, difficulty standing card, war disability card or European disabled parking badge.

For guests from outside France, the following are accepted: disability card, European disabled parking badge or a medical certificate (stating the person has a disability in French or English, signed and stamped by a doctor and issued within the last 3 months).

The **Easy Access Card** is for guests with temporary or debilitating illnesses or injuries (that have not led to them being registered as disabled). The Easy Access Card is also available for expectant mothers. It acts in the same way as the Priority Card, giving you access via a specially adapted entrance. This card does not officially offer priority access, but the result is similar to the Priority Card.

A medical certificate is required for this card. This certificate must state that the person has a debilitating illness, is temporarily disabled or is pregnant in French or English, signed and stamped by a doctor and issued within the last three months. Only one helper may accompany the disabled guest on attractions, unless they have a *carte de priorité familiale* in which case all helpers named on the card may board with the disabled person.

Additional information: When a disabled person presents themselves at Guest Relations to ask for a Priority or Easy Access card, they are asked questions to determine their degree of handicap and which rides will be accessible to them. For example, someone who cannot transfer out of a wheelchair may not ride *Pirates of the Caribbean*.

As well as the card itself, you will be given a copy of the Accessibility Guide with detailed information on each attraction. You can also consult this in advance at www.bit.ly/dlpdisab before your trip.

Some attractions require that guests with Priority or Easy Access cards (and with certain disabilities) make a reservation at the ride entrance and return later. Organised character meet and greets usually use a reservation system, and there will be a Cast Member with characters to reserve a slot for you.

Some attractions may not be accessible to guests with certain disabilities. In this case, family members cannot use the card in place of the disabled person – they must use the standby queue or Fastpass, if available.

Certain disabilities may require that the disabled person be accompanied to ride.

Pregnant mothers may not ride certain attractions for their safety and will politely be refused access.

Features for Guests with Disabilities

Hearing-impaired visitors: Disney Park information points, as well as some Walt Disney Studios Park attractions, are equipped with induction loops to assist guests. These attractions are: *CinéMagique, Animagique Theatre, Disney Junior Live on Stage!, Stitch Live!* and *The Twilight Zone: Tower of Terror*.

Mobility impaired visitors: Cast Members cannot escort or help disabled guests to attractions. They will, of course, provide directions and assist inside attractions.

Some attractions require that disabled guests transfer from their wheelchair to an attraction vehicle. For these attractions, disabled guests must be accompanied by at least one non-disabled adult (18+) to assist. Cast Members may not help visitors in or out of their wheelchair or ride vehicles. For some attractions, visitors must be ambulatory.

In Walt Disney Studios Park, all attraction queues are wheelchair accessible; this is also the case for *Buzz Lightyear Laser Blast, Princess Pavilion* and *Meet Mickey Mouse* in Disneyland Park. For attractions where this is not the case, a Priority Card allows guests entry via a separate entrance.

A designated viewing area for guests in wheelchairs is available for the parade, *Disney Illuminations* and stage shows.

All toilets have accessible areas for visitors with reduced mobility.

Unisex toilets (with cubicles so a carer may join wheelchair users) are available in every land of Disneyland Park. They are also available at *Moteurs… Action! Stunt Show Spectacular* in Walt Disney Studios Park during performances.

All shops and Table Service restaurants are accessible. At Quick Service places, ask a Cast Member for assistance if necessary.

An accessible shuttle bus is available between all Disney hotels (except Davy Crockett Ranch) and the theme parks. Ask at the hotel desk, the Disney Express desk in *Marne La Vallée – Chessy* station, or Guest Services in the parks for details and to book this free service.

Hotels each have rooms adapted to meet the needs of guests in wheelchairs. These have an extra-large bathroom with a bath, handrails and a raised toilet. Additionally, mobility-impaired guests can hire a seat to help them to wash without assistance (to be requested when making the reservation). The bedroom door has a spy hole at wheelchair height in accessible rooms. Bathrooms at Davy Crockett Ranch, Sequoia Lodge and Santa Fe Hotels have a shower suitable for mobility-impaired guests.

Visually impaired guests:
At some attractions, a companion may need to describe the surroundings. Some attractions and areas of the park are dimly lit.

At hotels, Disney recommends that visually impaired guests inform the hotel reception of their visual impairment upon arrival. A Cast Member will show guests to their room, and show them around the rest of the Disney hotel so that visually impaired guests

can orientate themselves. Telephones and television remotes with large buttons, as well as room keys with Braille, may be requested when making a reservation or at reception upon arrival.

Guide Dogs:
Guide and assistant dogs are allowed in the parks and on certain attractions. On attractions where dogs are not permitted, they must be left with a helper. Dogs may not be left unattended or with a Cast Member. Visually impaired guests may need to be accompanied on certain attractions. If bringing a guide dog, there must be at least two helpers with a disabled guest – one to accompany the guest, and another to take care of the guide dog.

Food Allergies:
Disneyland Paris offers allergen-free meals at selected restaurants. We recommend warning your hotel so an allergen-free breakfast can be prepared. When booking Table Service meals, state your allergies. Review Disneyland Paris' allergen guide at www.bit.ly/dlpallergy.

Other information:
Cast Members may refuse guests access to attractions for safety or other reasons.

Some attractions only accept one disabled guest at a time for safety and legal reasons. In these cases, the wait for a disabled guest can be as long or longer than the standard queue line.

Guests with medication that must be kept cool may leave it at one of the First Aid points in the two parks or Disney Village.

For safety reasons, all visitors: with reduced mobility or visual impairment, with a cognitive or mental health disorder, with behaviour disorder or autism or with a learning disability, must be accompanied by at least one non-disabled companion over the age of 18 to assist them. Some attractions allow helpers to accompany several people with disabilities (details are in the Disney Accessibility Guide).

Some attractions may have low-light areas, flashing lights or loud sound effects, dropping floors and other effects. Companions should pay particular attention to all these factors when preparing for the stay and should read the safety information available at the entrance to each attraction, as well as the Disney Parks Accessibility Guide.

Disneyland Paris for Walt Disney World Regulars

Many guests visit Disneyland Paris after having visited the Walt Disney World Resort in Florida. Both resorts immerse you in the Disney magic, but it is important to understand that the two locations are very different. This chapter helps you compare and contrast.

The Cast Members and Languages

The Cast Members in Florida and California, for the most part, go above and beyond, are incredibly polite, are never rude to a guest, have a passion for Disney and do everything to make your stay as magical as possible.

However, the Cast Members in the US are very restricted by the Disney rulebook, which even affects their personal lives such as how they can cut and style their hair.

Disneyland Paris is a Disney Park for the 21st century where a 'Disney Look' dictating employees personal appearance is illegal. French employment laws are stringent, so Cast Members cannot be reprimanded for not smiling or for leaning at work.

In addition, French customer service is very different to that in the USA. Having said this, most of the Paris Cast are pleasant, inviting and helpful – just do not expect American standards in France.

Cast Members in Paris generally speak several languages, and having a chat with one of the Cast could lead to you booking your next vacation to somewhere you would never have thought of visiting.

All Cast Members must speak at least two major European languages, one of which must be French.

Almost the entire Cast speak English well, but it is not mandatory. You may, on a rare occasion, encounter a Cast Member that does not speak English, so it pays to learn some basic French.

It is basic manners to learn some of the language when visiting another country and at least say *Bonjour* and *Merci.*

Local Customs

According to the latest available figures from Disneyland Paris, 48% of all visitors to the resort are French, and 16% are from the UK. Other countries with a high number of guests include Spain and Italy.

Disneyland Paris has a very high proportion of European visitors, unlike Walt Disney World's visitors from all corners of the world (but mainly Americans).

Many American customs do not apply to a European audience. For example, many Europeans do not queue in daily life. Instead, people gather in small groups instead of an orderly queue. For example, when a bus arrives, it is a free-for-all and people rush for the doors with no regard for those waiting for the longest.

During random character appearances in the parks, you can expect a crowd of parents pushing their children to get their photo taken first. When a queue is set up, though, Europeans seem to be fine at complying.

Tipping is also different. Meals in France have a tip included in the price so there is no need to tip (although a small tip is appreciated). This compares to the US, where tips of 15% or 20% of a meal's price are expected.

In general, guests are much less respectful at the Parisian parks – they enter cordoned off areas, sit anywhere they can, and smoke freely in the parks despite it being banned.

Guests in Europe expect to have an alcoholic beverage with their meal – as such, you will find beer on sale at Quick Service locations. Wine and other alcoholic drinks are also offered at all Table Service locations.

In general, Europeans are more used to drinking alcohol with a meal than Americans; the sale of alcoholic drinks has not harmed the parks.

Lastly, the European audience is a little bit more fashion-conscious than the crowds that visit Florida. Ponchos, for example, are sold at Disneyland Paris, but they are often replaced by umbrellas and raincoats in Europe instead. Having said this, there is more than a fair share of guests dressed "interestingly" at Disneyland Paris.

Weather

Florida is known as the "sunshine state", and you can expect temperatures to reach 30°C (80-90°F) for much of the year. There are occasions where there are cold snaps and the temperature drops for a few days, but nothing to the levels seen in Paris.

Paris' weather is much more variable; the average daily temperature in

Paris in July and August is about 25°C (77°F) whereas temperatures in January and February average at 3°CC (37°F), often dipping below freezing. In the summer, it is usual for a few days to exceed 37°C (100°F) in Paris.

Visitors to Walt Disney World have to deal with Hurricane season much of the year (June to

November) when weather can get extreme, and hurricanes are possible. These are not usual in Paris.

Orlando visitors also deal with a tropical climate with daily thunderstorms in the summer, closing all outdoor attractions and drenching anyone not prepared. Paris' rain is more unpredictable, and is present year-round - thunderstorms are rare.

Resort Size and Transportation

The size difference between the two resorts is staggering: Walt Disney World is 47 square miles or 121 square kilometres. In comparison, Disneyland Paris is 22.3 square kilometres.

From the furthest resort hotelsto the parks is no more than a 20-minute walk at Disneyland Paris or a five-minute bus journey.

However, at Walt Disney World most journeys cannot be walked - not only because of the distance but because there are no pavements connecting most areas due to the sprawling size of Walt Disney World.

At Disneyland Paris, the two theme parks are within walking distance, as is the Disney Village. Everything is a bus journey away from each other at Walt Disney World.

The advantage of Disneyland Paris' small size is that you can walk throughout the whole resort, you can visit any of the other hotels easily, and you will spend less time travelling and more time enjoying yourself. The disadvantage is that there are fewer things to do: no water parks, fewer hotels, and crucially fewer theme parks (there are two in Paris, versus four in Florida).

Looking at the parks, Disneyland Park is slightly bigger than Magic Kingdom Park, but with emptier, quieter areas and fewer rides. Park walkways feel significantly less crowded in Paris.

Walt Disney Studios Park in Paris is about half the size of Disney's Hollywood Studios in Orlando. The resort hotels in Paris are also generally smaller than their Floridian counterparts.

If you have visited Disneyland Resort in California, Disneyland Paris is much more comparable to it – everything is within walking distance. Paris' resort is larger than the Disneyland Resort, however.

The area where Disneyland Paris is located is as much a major transport hub, as it is a world-class theme park resort. On Disneyland Paris property, just two minutes from the park entrances, you can hop on a high-speed train to travel across France, or even to the UK.

Alternatively, you can use the regional trains and travel into central Paris in just 35 minutes. You can also drive and be at non-Disney locations in just a few minutes too.

Disneyland Paris is all very self-contained, so if you do fancy escaping the magic, it is easy to do - unlike in Florida! For some people, this freedom is a benefit, though others prefer the Floridian immersion of the Disney magic that lets them forget about the outside world.

Pricing

Disney trips can be very pricey when you take into account all of the costs.

Room prices at on-site hotels include tickets to the theme parks for the length of stay. However, you will not find a room at a Disney hotel for under €220 per night – and these are the cheapest rooms at off-peak seasons.

In contrast, the cheapest hotels in Walt Disney World are half this price, though park tickets are not included. At Disneyland Paris, there are almost always special offers available, so do not book at full rate.

A one-day entry ticket to Disneyland Paris for one park is €87 (£78 or $98) for adults and €80 for children. A two-park hopper is €107 (£96 or $120) and €100 respectively. The daily rate drastically reduces the longer you visit the resort. A 4-day ticket is €249 (£223 or $279) for adults. You can get discounted tickets online, however.

For comparison, at Walt Disney World, a one day,

one park adult ticket is $116 to $169 dollars with tax, or a park hopper (for four theme parks) is $180 to $233. A 4-day ticket is $426-$597 for one park per day, or $532-$704 with the park hopper option).

Walt Disney World tickets are substantially more expensive. Although there are more activities in the Floridian parks, the 4-day hopper costs twice the price per person.

Longer stays of 7 or 14-days in Florida become more affordable per day.

Food prices at Disneyland Paris, however, are slightly more expensive in comparison to the US and many people bring picnic food into the parks for this reason.

A burger, fries and drink combo will set you back about €15 (£13.50/$17) at Disneyland Paris. A burger and fries in the US will cost you about $12 without a drink, or about $15 with one.

At Table Service establishments, the price difference is even more notable. A Set Menu at a good in-park restaurant will set you back €50 to €60 ($60 to $72) at Disneyland Paris. The equivalent at Walt Disney World would be about 30% cheaper.

This adds up to a big price difference when ordering for a family of four over several days.

Don't expect signature foods like Dole Whips and Mickey Premium Bars in Disneyland Paris, either.

Fastpass

Fastpass at Disneyland Paris is a paper system (the same as Walt Disney World's previous system). You go to a Fastpass machine, insert your ticket and get a return time.

Walt Disney World has a digital Fastpass+ system. With Fastpass+ you can make ride reservations on your smartphone or using in-park kiosks up to 60 days in advance, or on the day

itself.

Another difference is that at Disneyland Paris, the return time windows are only 30 minutes long instead of the 1 hour in the US parks.

Unique Attractions and Details

Disneyland Paris has many unique rides and shows which cannot be found at Walt Disney World.

In Disneyland Park, *Phantom Manor* is a beautiful rendition of the classic Haunted Mansion ride with a new storyline and an entirely different interior but keeping some familiar elements.

Pirates of the Caribbean is much longer, has a better queue, new scenes and bigger drops in Paris.

Star Wars Hyperspace Mountain is beautiful in Paris from the outside - it is an intense looping roller Coaster inside that blows its Floridian counterpart out of the water; *Big Thunder Mountain* is great fun in Paris and is set in the middle of an island.

Furthermore, there are lots of unique walkthroughs such as *The Nautilus* and *Alice's Curious Labyrinth* too. *Casey Junior* and *Storybook Canal Boats* also do not exist in Florida.

Indiana Jones et le Temple du Peril is also a unique roller Coaster. There is, however, no 'New Fantasyland expansion' in Paris.

The *Disney Illuminations* night-time spectacular is not too dissimilar to Magic Kingdom's *Happily Ever After* show.

In Walt Disney Studios Park, *Crush's Coaster* is a unique spinning roller Coaster in the dark, and *Cars Quatre Roues Rallye* is a unique tea-cup style ride themed to *Cars*.

The *Art of Disney Animation* exists in Paris after it was shuttered in Florida – the same applies to *Studio Tram Tour*.

Toy Story Playland has three unique rides, and *Animagique* Theatre is home to a unique stage show. *Stitch Live* is a cool interactive show, similar to Turtle Talk with Crush.

Finally, *Ratatouille: The Adventure* is a world-class, dark ride unlike anything in the US parks.

Disneyland Park is beautiful. Everything is incredibly elaborately themed, sharing inspiration from the US parks while introducing exotic elements that cannot be found elsewhere.

In comparison, Walt Disney

Studios Park is filled with concrete and metallic structures everywhere, with very few thematic details. Although over the past five years there has been an effort to improve the park, it is clear that Walt Disney Studios Park lacks the detail that makes Disney theme parks unique.

Even Hollywood Studios, which is (in our opinion) the worst-themed park at Walt Disney World, has superior theming to the Studios park in Paris. The number of attractions at both the Studios parks is paltry, though the Floridian park is receiving several new attractions - an expansion will arrive shortly in Paris.

The hotels at Disneyland Paris are American-themed but do not live up to the resort hotels found at Walt Disney World. The hotels in Paris are just hotels, whereas you could spend several days at the hotel resorts in the US and enjoy the surroundings and experiences on offer.

The Seasons and The Future

Disneyland Paris offers its guests something different throughout the year, with seasonal and special events that celebrate traditions such as St. Patrick's Day, Halloween and Christmas. This section explores all of these. Then, we take a look at the future of the resort.

Season of the Force

January to March 2020

The Season of the Force returns to Disneyland Paris in 2020. Information about the event has not yet been released, though the following is what took place in 2019. We expect the new event to be broadly similar.

"Star Wars: A Galactic Celebration" Nighttime Show - Make your way to Walt Disney Studios Park for a sensational show in front of Hollywood Tower Hotel, as light projection, special effects and live characters turn darkness into spectacular scenes from the Star Wars saga. This "360-degree" show will provide "perfect immersion" in the Star Wars Universe.

Expect to see Chewbacca, R2-D2, Kylo Ren, Darth Maul, Darth Vader and more in person during this show.

"Star Wars: A Galaxy Far, Far Away" Stage Show - Let the Force guide you to Production Courtyard in Walt Disney Studios Park for an extraordinary example of galactic might. Will you submit to the dark side? Or does your path lead to the light side?

This show puts the spotlight on several iconic characters from the saga, such as Darth Vader and Kylo Ren, to name but a few.

Stormtrooper March - Blast off to Walt Disney Studios Park and witness the wicked wonder of Captain Phasma leading a battalion of stormtroopers on an iconic military march - and they're on the hunt for rebel spies.

St. David's Welsh Festival

6th to 8th March 2020

This three-day-long mini-season has been traditionally celebrated in Frontierland, at Disneyland Park.

During the festival, guests can take photos with some of their favourite Disney characters clad in traditional Welsh robes.

In addition, Disneyland Paris usually has traditional Welsh singers, such as a choir, perform at the festival several times throughout the day.

Traditional music, a crafts market, traditional food and drink, complimentary face painting, and a special St. David's fireworks display make the festival a fun and unique event.

St. Patrick's Day

17th March 2020

Much like the St. David's Day celebrations on the previous page, this one-day celebration of all things Celtic takes place in Frontierland, at Disneyland Park.

Guests can enjoy live traditional music, photo opportunities, character appearances, a pre-parade, and a special St. Patrick's Day fireworks display.

Disneyland Paris MagicRun Weekend

19th to 22nd September 2019 / 2020 date to be conf.

The following applies to the 2019 event - we expect the 2020 event to be broadly similar.

• **5km Run** (20th September 2019) – A 5km run from 8:00pm. The race goes through Walt Disney Studios Park with characters along the route. Ages 5 and up.

• **Kids Races** (21st September 2019) – Kids races take place from 11:00am or 3:00pm for children under 12. There are 100m, 200m and 1km races.

• **10km Run** (21st September 2019) – This 10km run will take place exclusively inside Disneyland Paris grounds with characters en-route.

• **Half Marathon** (22nd September 2019) – The main 21.1km half-marathon starts at 7:00am. It goes through both theme parks, hotels, as well as the local

villages around the theme parks. Disney characters are stationed throughout the route. The Half Marathon race is open to ages 18+ only and a medical certificate is required.

• **RunDisney Health & Fitness Expo** – From 19th to 21st September 2019 in the Disney Events Arena. Here participants can get their race T-shirt, race number bib and gear bags. Plus, everyone can see the latest in fitness apparel, footwear, sunglasses, gadgets, and nutritional products.

The Expo also showcases a Speaker Series with appearances by celebrity runners and seminars on training, running, and nutrition featuring speakers and panellists from the running industry.

Race participants receive a medal for each

race completed and refreshments during and after their race. Special medials are available for those who complete multiple races.

Travel package bookings are sold which include hotel stays, park tickets and the race entry.

Race-only prices for 2019 are: €77 for the half-marathon, €59 for the 10km, €40 for the 5km and €15 for the kids run. A race-only Photopass is available for €29-€45, and a 'race plus park' Photopass is €79.

Halloween

October 2019 and October 2020

Disneyland Paris' Halloween season is one of the most elaborate celebrations at the resort, with unique shows, parades, décors and more to delight guests.

This information is for the 2018 Halloween season. Some events may not return for the 2019 and 2020 season, and new events may be added, but this sets expectations as Halloween is broadly similar each year. Details are usually released six weeks before the event.

"It's Good to Be Bad" – See the Disney Villains out in full force in this show on the Royal Castle Stage.

Decorations, Food and Merchandise – Frontierland is invaded by ghostly decorations for some great photo opportunities. Disney characters also sport Halloween-themed costumes. Villains-themed merchandise and special Halloween inspired menus are available.

Character Meets – Keep your eyes peeled for meet and greets with José Carioca and Panchito Pistoles, Donald's sidekicks in the film The Three Caballeros. Mickey and Minnie will also make an appearance for truly splendid meet 'n' greets. And if you like witches, you'll love Daisy's costume!

Disney's Halloween Party (2019 info):
On 26th and 31st October between 8:00pm and 2:00am, this ticketed event offers an evening of frightening entertainment.

Most Disneyland Park attractions are open during the event and guests may wear Halloween costumes (subject to restrictions).

Entry is €69 for the party on 26th October and €79 for 31st October for guests aged 3 and up. Under 3s go free. Guests may enter from 5:00pm with party tickets.

Unique entertainment is available during the party including character meet and greets, special shows and lots of exclusive party-only entertainment.

Mickey's Magical Fireworks and Bonfire

4th, 6th & 8th November 2010

See the night sky transformed above Lake Disney as Disney sets its fireworks off to music to celebrate Bonfire Night. The show lasts approximately 20 minutes.

Lake Disney is located by the on-site Disney hotels - no park entry is required and admission is free.

Christmas

Mid-November 2019 to early January 2020

For the most magical time of the year, make Disneyland Paris your stop. Here you are guaranteed snow every day, magical characters and unforgettable experiences.

The following details are for the 2018 Christmas season. Traditionally, the Christmas seasons do not change hugely from year to year so you can expect much of this information to be valid for the 2019 and 2020 Christmas seasons too. Information on the 2019 season will not be unveiled before September 2019 at the earliest.

The park will be filled with Christmas touches everywhere you go but no more so than Main Street, U.S.A - here you will find a giant Christmas tree, snowmen on each corner and baubles and tinsel abound.

Show: A Merry Stitchmas – Stitch will be leading

the event on the Sleeping Beauty Castle stage. Mickey, Minnie and their friends will teach Stitch the meaning of Christmas through songs. Are you ready to feel the beat of a super fun Christmas?

Nighttime Show: Goofy's Incredible Christmas – Get ready for an immersive night-time experience that uses mapping technology and breathtaking special effects to transform a cult attraction – The Twilight

Zone Tower of Terror.

Goofy will light up the show in true Christmas spirit. He'll take you on a journey over spectacular landscapes, from the North Pole to the most extravagant party you could possibly imagine.

Show: Mickey's Christmas Big Band – Gather your friends and family and make your way to Animagique in Walt Disney Studios Park for this cracking Broadway tap dancing show. Get into the Christmas spirit and tap, tap, tap along to some classic carols – all while Mickey works his magic on the drums.

Show: Surprise for Mickey – Can you keep a secret? Minnie has planned a very special Christmas surprise for The World's Biggest Mouse Party. And you're invited!

Disney's Christmas Parade – This Christmas-themed parade marches down Fantasyland and Main Street, U.S.A. The parade stars Father Christmas until Christmas day. The regular parade, *Disney Stars on Parade* is also performed once daily during the Christmas season.

Mickey's Magical Christmas Lights – Every evening as the night falls, the park's signature Christmas tree comes to life with the help of Mickey, Minnie and Santa in this illumination ceremony. The show takes place daily.

Meet Characters – You can meet both Santa and Mickey at *Meet Mickey Mouse*. There are two queue lines – one for Mickey photos and the other for Santa photos. You'll also have the chance to meet Marie from the Aristocats, Scrooge McDuck, Thumper, Miss Bunny and more throughout the park!

Special Dinners – In Europe, Christmas Eve and New Year's Eve dinners are a big family affair. As such, dinners on these days are available at a heavy supplement.

Prices vary from €129 to €259 per adult on Christmas Eve. On Christmas day a special 4-course lunch is available for about €180 per adult. New Year's Eve meals range in price from €119 to €299 per adult.

Full details on these meals are available over the phone.

Personally, we think these prices are very high with a family of 4 spending at least €400 on a single meal. Our recommendation is to eat in one of the Quick Service restaurants to avoid these hefty price tags (or at a Table Service location as a late lunch).

Alternatively, choose from one of the Table Service restaurants not doing special dinners, or eat in the Disney Village at selected restaurants. Reservations are strongly recommended.

New Year's Eve

31st December 2019

Celebrate the start of the New Year at Disneyland Paris.

This is traditionally the busiest day at the resort and you can expect the theme parks to reach maximum capacity with very long wait times for all rides.

If you can put up with that, you can experience a fireworks display at Walt Disney Studios Park or at Lake Disney (no admission cost at this last location).

Walt Disney Studios is open until 1:00am meaning you have one hour of post-fireworks attraction time.

All the Christmas entertainment is still running on this date and continues into early January.

New Year's Eve Party: Disneyland Paris promises a star-studded evening packed with surprises. Enjoy The Incredible New Year's Eve Parade. Above Sleeping Beauty Castle, the New Year fireworks will amaze, and why not take to the dance floor or enjoy a whole host of other surprises?

This is a ticketed party - tickets are €99 per guest and allow entry from 5:00pm to 2:00am - the park is open for ticket holders only starting from 8:00pm.

The Future - Projects in Progress & Rumours

Walt Disney Studios Park Expansion – Walt Disney Studios Park is set to continue to expand in size, and with additional attractions - Disney is investing €2 Billion into the theme park in total.

Construction has already started and the project is expected to open in three phrases from 2021 until 2025.

The three new areas coming to the park are:

• Marvel area including a new Iron Man roller-coaster, a possible Spider-Man interactive ride, and marvel character meet and greet
• Frozen area with one new ride
• Star Wars area with one new ride

•Disney says: "In addition to the three new areas, the creative vision includes a new lake, which will be the focal point for entertainment experiences and will also connect each of the new park areas."

Disney Village expansion – Disney Village is set to be expanded over the coming years, with new shopping and dining experiences.

Technological updates –

Free public Wi-Fi is due to be introduced at the parks, and in future the Fastpass system may even go digital, doing away with paper tickets.

Hotels – Disneyland Paris has been refurbishing all of its hotels over the past few years. Hotel New York is closed for a complete overhaul, and this will be followed by the Disneyland Hotel soon.

In addition, there are plans for a new "value"-priced on-site hotel. Construction has not started on this, so this is still many years off.

A Special Thanks

Thank you very much for reading our travel guide. We hope this book has made a big difference to your trip to Disneyland Paris, and that you have found some tips that will save you time, money and hassle! Remember to take this guide with you when you are visiting the resort. This guide is also available in a digital format.

If you have any feedback about any element of the guide, or have noticed changes in the parks that differ from what is in the book, do let us know by sending us a message. To contact us, visit our website at www.independentguidebooks.com.

If you enjoyed the guide, we would love for you to leave a review on Amazon or wherever you have purchased this guide. Your reviews make a huge difference in helping other people find this guide. Thank you.

Have a magical time!

If you have enjoyed this guide, other travel guides in this series include:

- The Independent Guide to Walt Disney World
- The Independent Guide to Universal Orlando
- The Independent Guide to Universal Studios Hollywood
- The Independent Guide to Disneyland
- The Independent Guide to Hong Kong
- The Independent Guide to Tokyo
- The Independent Guide to Dubai
- The Independent Guide to Paris
- The Independent Guide to London
- The Independent Guide to New York City

Photo credits:

The following photos have been used from Flickr (unless otherwise stated) in this guide under a Creative Commons license. Thank you to: Disneyland Hotel (cover) - Edgardo W. Olivera; Tower of Terror (cover) - David Jafra; Eurostar (small) - 'kismihok; Eurostar (large) - Philip Sheldrake; Thunder Mesa Riverboat, Blanche Neige and La Cabane des Robinson, Newport bay close, Dumbo, Phantom Manor, Indiana Jones, Peter Pan, it's a small world, Wild West Show - Loren Javier; Dumbo & Pinocchio - Jeremy Thompson; Nautilus - Paul Beattie; Star Tours - Anna Fox; and Ratatouille exterior - Eleazar; Fastpass (single) - Joel; Fastpass (multiple) - JJ Merelo; View of Lake Disney (La Marina section) - Nicola; Val d'EOPE - Tves Jalabert; Davy Crockett's Adventure - aventure-aventure.com; Golf - DisneylandParis.com; Aerial Image - Apple Maps; Disney Dollars - R Reeves; Teacups - Kabayanmark Images; Newport Bay far - Nicola; New York Hotel - .Martin.; Crush parade float - Moto@Club4AG; Sleeping Beauty Castle - Sergey Galyonkin; BTM and Halloween- Kevin Marshall; Tower of Terror - Ken Lund; Ratatouille - Martin Lewison; Parachute Drop - Ludovic; Panoramagique - Victor R Ruiz; Eiffel Tower - Pedro Szekely;.

Some images are copyright The Walt Disney Company, Disneyland Paris and EuroDisney SCA.

Disneyland Park Map

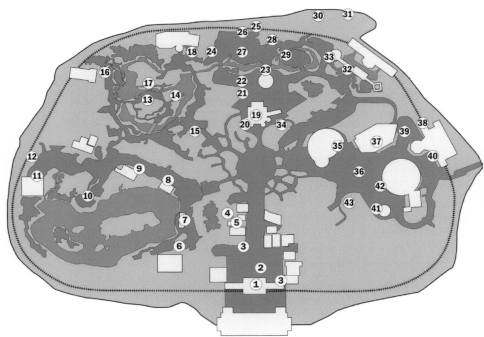

1 - Main Street, U.S.A. Station
2 - Horse-Drawn Streetcars
3 - Main Street Vehicles
4 - Liberty Arcade (Statue of Liberty Tableau)
5 - Dapper Dan's Hair Cuts
6 - Phantom Manor
7 - Thunder Mesa Riverboat Landing
8 - Rustler Roundup Shooting Gallery
9 - Big Thunder Mountain
10 - Pocahontas Indian Village
11 - Frontierland Theatre
12 - Frontierland Station
13 - La Cabane des Robinson (Treehouse)
14 - Pirates' Beach
15 - Le Passage Enchante d'Aladdin
16 - Indiana Jones et le Temple du Peril
17 - Adventure Isle
18 - Pirates of the Caribbean
19 - Sleeping Beauty Castle
20 - Dragon's Lair
21 - Snow White and the Seven Dwarfs
22 - Pinocchio's Fantastic Journey
23 - Lancelot's Carousel
24 - Peter Pan's Flight
25 - Fantasyland Station
26 - Meet Mickey
27 - Dumbo: The Flying Elephant
28 - Alice's Curious Labyrinth
29 - Mad Hatter's Tea Cups
30 - Casey Jr.
31 - Storybook Canal Boats
32 - "it's a small world"
33 - Princess Pavilion
34 - Castle Stage
35 - Buzz Lightyear Laser Blast
36 - Orbitron
37 - Videopolis
38 - Discoveryland Station
39 - Star Tours
40 - Discoveryland Theatre
41 - Nautilus
42 - Star Wars Hyperspace Mountain
43 - Autopia

Walt Disney Studios Park Map

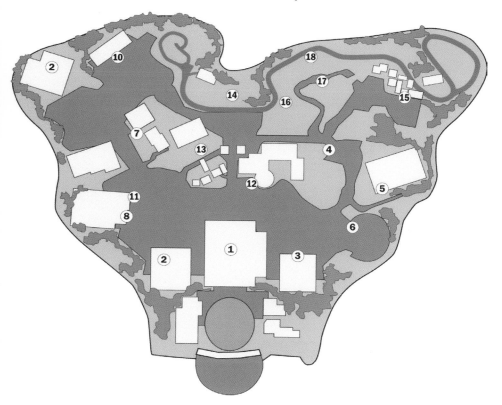

1 - Disney Studio 1
2 - CineMagique Theatre
3 - Animagique Theatre
4 - Cars Race Rallye
5 - Crush's Coaster
6 - Flying Carpets over Agrabah
7 - CLOSED.
8 - CLOSED.
9 - Rock 'n' Roller Coaster: Starring Aerosmith (Closing Sep 2019)
10 - Moteurs...Action! Stunt Show Spectacular

11 - Stitch Live!
12 - Animation Celebration
13 - The Twilight Zone: Tower of Terror
14 - Studio Tram Tour: Behind the Magic
15 - Ratatouille: The Adventure
16 - Toy Soldiers Parachute Drop
17 - Slinky Dog Zig Zag Spin
18 - RC Racer

Printed in Great Britain
by Amazon

35065642R00061